Miracles Do Happen

Miracles Do Happen

Sister Briege McKenna, O.S.C.
with
Henry Libersat

St. Martin's Press
New York

Library of Congress Cataloging-in-Publication Data

McKenna, Briege.
        Miracles do happen.

        1. Spiritual healing.   2. Christian life—Catholic
authors.   3. McKenna, Briege,   I. Libersat, Henry.
II. Title.
BT732.5.M43   1989   234'.13   88-29847
ISBN 0-312-02606-9

First published in The United States by Servant Books.

To

Sister Helen Conway, OSC
Mrs. Margie Grace
Miss Colette Scallon

Miracles Do Happen is a book about Sister Briege's special relationship with Jesus and the way he has ministered to his people through her. The marvellous stories Briege tells in her own inimitable way contain profound teachings on many Catholic beliefs, beliefs often challenged today, even within the church itself. I pray this book will be an inspiration and source of encouragement for all those who seek to follow Jesus.
—Sister Margaret McGill
    Abbess General of the Sisters of St. Clare

Contents

The purpose of this book:

In his disciples' presence, Jesus performed many other miracles which are not written down in this book. But these have been written in order that you may believe that Jesus is the Messiah, the Son of God, and through your faith in him you may have life. (Jn 20:30-31)

Foreword

THIS IS A BOOK ABOUT the ministry a woman can have in the Roman Catholic church today. It is like no other book that has ever been written on that topic, for the simple reason that no other woman has ever had the kind of ministry that Sister Briege McKenna has had for the past ten years or so. At a time when a good many Catholic women have been seeking the right to be ordained and to share in the ministry of priests, Sister Briege has been exercising a ministry to priests and for priests, to such great numbers of them, and in so many parts of the world, that I have no hesitation in asserting that no woman has ever touched and changed the lives of so many priests as she has done. And I am grateful to be able to say that I am one of them.

I first came to know Sister Briege about ten years ago when we happened to be together as members of a team giving a retreat to priests in Scotland. The following year we were both members of a team giving a retreat to priests in the United States. A year or two later I received an invitation to give a retreat to priests working in Japan, during the month of November. The man who wrote asked me to suggest the names of some other retreat directors who might help with this retreat, since they expected as many as one hundred priests to attend it. I suggested the names of three priests whom I know, and then, since I had been so deeply impressed by Briege's ministry at the other retreats, I suggested her name as well, adding that I had no idea whether this would go over well in Japan.

As it turned out, none of the priests I had named was available, so they tried to get in touch with Briege. But there was a mix-up in communication, so that it was several months before this request reached her. In the meanwhile, her mother general had asked her not to take on any commitments for the month of November that year, as she had something in mind for her to do at that time. So Briege had been turning down all kinds of requests for ministry during November. The very day her mother general told her that plans had been changed and that she would no longer need her was the day she finally received the request to help with the retreat in Japan. I have no doubt that all this was because the Lord knew there were priests in Japan who needed her special kind of ministry—but I feel that he arranged it for my benefit as well.

It is a wonderful—and very humbling—experience for a priest to work so closely with Sister Briege McKenna in her unique ministry to priests. There were things, of course, that only I could do, like celebrating mass and giving absolution in the sacrament of reconciliation. There were other things that both of us did about equally well, like giving the retreat talks. But then there was her own special ministry, using the gifts the Lord has given her, that I could only witness and marvel at. I mean her gift of listening to the priests, most of them missionaries, almost all of them years older than herself, as they brought their very personal needs, whether spiritual or physical, to her so that she might pray with them. And I mean her gift of bringing their needs to the Lord in her simple, direct way of talking to Jesus; in many cases receiving a reply from the Lord in the form of an image or a word to share with them, and then sending them away consoled, renewed, in many cases healed in body as well as in spirit.

I have often told my friends, more than half seriously, that it's easy to give a retreat with Briege, because she hears most of the confessions. It's true she can't give absolution, but it's also true that if someone she prays with really needs absolution, he will come to celebrate the sacrament of reconciliation already profoundly reconciled with the Lord.

As anyone who reads this book will realize, Sister Briege is a person who puts Jesus first in her life, and her greatest gift is her ability to bring others to want to put him first too. She is truly a "signpost to Jesus." As she says in this book: "It is the Lord who does wonders. I am convinced that no one can do more than become a signpost that points to him, to help others discover him in their hearts and permit him to give them great blessings." True enough—no one can do more than this. But I don't know anyone who does it quite as well as Briege McKenna does.

Francis A. Sullivan, S.J.

Acknowledgments

For many years people have been asking me to write this book. I always felt that it would be done in the Lord's own time. Now is the acceptable time, as Saint Paul says.

Many people have prayed for me and supported me with their prayers and encouragement. However, a number of people deserve a special expression of my gratitude.

I am grateful to Sister Margaret McGill, mother general of the Congregation of the Sisters of St. Clare, and to Sister Helen Conway, the former mother general, for their constant encouragement and support.

Special thanks, too, to my bishop, W. Thomas Larken of St. Petersburg and Msgr. Laurence Higgins, my pastor in Tampa, for their understanding and guidance.

Cardinal Leon Joseph Suenens of Belgium has been tremendous in providing me with clear direction and a faithful overview of the growth of the spiritual movements in the universal church.

Veronica O'Brien, also of Belgium, has inspired me with her vision and devotion to spreading the Catholic faith and has encouraged me with her friendship and prayers.

My religious sisters at St. Lawrence Convent, Tampa, deserve much gratitude for their joyful response to the demands made of them by living with a person whose phone never ceases to ring. My entire community, worldwide, have been generous in their prayers and support.

Father Kevin Scallon, my co-worker in evangelization and priests' retreats, has taught me so much about the priesthood and inspired me with his great love for the church and his faithfulness to his commitment as a priest.

Father Frank Sullivan, S.J., who has written the foreword for this book, has for many years been a tremendous inspiration to me and has helped me achieve a balanced theological perspective. He has opened many doors to ministry, especially in Japan, that may not have opened without him.

Ingrid Orglmeister of Sao Paulo, Brazil, my interpreter, and her husband, Peter, have been friends for many years. Ingrid has been a great help in shedding light on the impact of my ministry in Brazil.

Peter and Margie Grace of Manhasset have most graciously provided much assistance to me in my travels and have opened their hearts and home to me. Margie, in many ways, has been like a mother; providing counsel and friendship.

Piet and Trude Derksen of The Netherlands have been steadfast in their support of Catholic ministry in Third World countries.

Special thanks to Doris and Francis Meagher of Clearwater, Florida whose home has become my home and whose love and friendship have been a great blessing and joy.

Linda and Joe Rooney of Florida graciously provided us with their beach home for the writing of *Miracles Do Happen*. I am grateful for their hospitality.

And I am grateful to Henry and Peg Libersat because *Miracles Do Happen* would not have happened without their support, talents, prayer, and time.

I thank all my many, many friends and acquaintances who make my ministry possible through their love and support.

Finally, Ann Spangler and the staff at Servant Books showed remarkable flexibility in helping us work within difficult schedules and in providing input and enthusiasm for this book.

ONE

Healed and Called

PENTECOST HAS ALWAYS BEEN a special day for me. Before I was born, my mother prayed for a girl; on Pentecost I was born.

On Christmas Day, 1959, when I was only thirteen years old my mother died suddenly. As I cried that night, I heard a voice say, "Don't worry, I'll take care of you." I didn't really understand that it was the Lord, but I felt peace. The next morning I knew I wanted to be a nun.

About a year and a half after my mother died, I went to the motherhouse of the Congregation of the Sisters of St. Clare in Newry, my home town in Ireland.

The sister who came to the door asked, "What can I do for you?"

"I want to see the Mother Abbess General," I said.

So she took me to see Mother Agnes O'Brien.

"Child, what is it?" the old nun asked.

"I want to be a nun," I said.

At that moment, in came the Abbess. "How old are you, child?"

"I'm fourteen and a bit," I said.

Mother Agnes, a very saintly nun, said to me, "We can't take you now. Canon law won't allow it. Come back later."

After some time, Mother Agnes asked me to come and stay with the woman who worked in the motherhouse, although I could not yet enter the novitiate. My father had to give permission for me to move to the convent. I still had not mentioned a word about this to him.

I went to ask him on a day in early June, as he was plowing in the field. He came over to the side of the field to sit with me. We chatted for a while and then I told him, "Daddy, I want to be a nun."

He said, "Well, if that's what you want, go ahead, and if it's not what you want, you'll know it."

Two days before my fifteenth birthday, the novice mistress came to me and said I was to enter the convent on my birthday. She told me to notify my father so that he could come.

My poor father, not really knowing anything about nuns, sent a telegram to my brother in England:

"Come quick. Briege entering convent. Might never see her again."

I was six months a postulant and then became a novice. My father came to the ceremonies. I first saw my daddy cry when my hair was cut off and all those curls came off.

When I made my first vows, on December 4, 1962, I had my first real spiritual experience. As I knelt in the chapel, waiting to be called up, I saw Jesus dressed as the Good Shepherd coming to me to take my hand, saying, "Come with me."

After several assignments in different convents, Mother Agnes, who was seriously ill, asked me to come and care for her. She had a great influence on my life. She had a great reverence for the priesthood and prayed for priests constantly. Although she never came to America, she founded our houses here. She told me much about the Sacred Heart and urged me to be a good, holy, and fervent religious.

Healing by the Power of the Holy Spirit

In 1964, I had developed severe pain in my feet. A doctor said it was caused by fallen arches and growing pains. But in 1965, an orthopedic surgeon diagnosed rheumatoid arthritis. I spent many months in a hospital in Belfast. Every night the sisters had to put plaster of paris boots on my feet, to try to prevent deformity. This was very painful.

One day, Mother Agnes called me to her bedside. She was leaving for the hospital. She told me she was going to die but that she would always pray for me—and she reminded me again, "Always stay close to Jesus."

I made my final profession on August 22, 1967, at the motherhouse in Newry. It was at that time that I volunteered to come to the United States. Although I volunteered, I cried for the two weeks prior to departure.

I arrived in Tampa, Florida, where I began teaching kindergarten that September. The climate had a bad effect on my condition and my arthritis worsened.

There was a doctor who said he could do very little for me but wanted to try out different medicines to see if they could help me. He prescribed all kinds of medicine. By 1968 I was on cortisone and took so much of it that it became ineffective. The pain was constant. As a side effect from the cortisone, I suffered lapses in my memory. I cried because of the pain. The doctor said there was no hope for me: I would be confined to a wheelchair. At that time I could still walk, but slowly and painfully.

I started to experience a great dryness in my spiritual life. I even began to ask myself whether I really believed in Jesus.

I didn't feel convinced of the power of the gospel. I didn't believe that Jesus would heal me. I believed that if I had gone to Lourdes or some other place there might be a healing, but I did not believe that healing could happen in normal daily living.

My soul was thirsting for the living God, but I didn't really know him. It was with this desire to know the Lord better that I went to my first prayer meeting. While I was afraid of the charismatic dimension, I was attracted to it because I saw people praying to Jesus as though he were right there. The Lord used my spiritual hunger to draw me to himself. I kept saying to myself, "There must be more to religious life and there must be more to Catholicism."

I had been good about "getting my prayers in," as a duty. But there was no joy in talking to the Lord, nor was I enthusiastic about witnessing to the power of the Lord.

However, one day before the Blessed Sacrament, I said, "Jesus, I'm going to find you, whatever it takes." That was really the beginning of my spiritual search.

In the process of seeking for a deeper meaning of my religious life and a deeper, more radical commitment to the Lord, I believe that Jesus gave me a spiritual healing. In December of 1970, I attended an ecumenical retreat in Orlando. I listened to talks on the power of prayer and the power of the Holy Spirit. I remember I had my shopping list of all the things I wanted from God—on my terms.

There was a priest at this prayer meeting. With my shopping list in mind, I thought, "Now if this priest would pray for me, I would get all these things." But physical healing was not on my list.

The Lord, as though he had read my mind, said to me, "Don't look at him, look at me." I remember looking at the clock as I closed my eyes. It was 9:15 A.M., December 9, 1970. The only prayer I said was "Jesus, please help me." At that moment, I felt a hand touch my head and thought it was the priest who had come over to me. I opened my eyes and no one was there, but there was a power going through my body. It's difficult to describe the feeling, but I often describe it this way: I felt like a banana being peeled.

I looked down. My fingers had been stiff, but not deformed like my feet. There had been sores on my elbows. I looked at myself. My fingers were limber, the sores were gone, and I could see that my feet, in sandals, were no longer deformed.

I jumped up screaming, "Jesus! You're right here!"

When Jesus showed himself to Thomas, all Thomas could

say was, "My Lord and my God!" When Jesus revealed himself to me that day, all I could say was "God! You're right here!" It was an act of faith in him.

Since that day I have never had arthritis and have been completely free of pain. That was the miraculous healing, but my inner life saw the greatest change.

Through the charismatic renewal, I experienced the release of the Holy Spirit. I had a new vision of the church, as though I was seeing the Eucharist and the sacrament of reconciliation through new glasses. I was seeing more clearly God's great love for us and what he has given us. Yet I still had one fear: healing. I was afraid of the sensational. When I was healed I said to myself, "I'm not going to tell anybody I've been healed because they will automatically attach healing power to it. They'll think I'm a healer now. Besides it's nobody's business. Why tell anybody?"

That was really protecting myself. I said, "I couldn't get involved in anything like that. I am a respectable member of a strict congregation."

I went from December of 1970 to June of 1971 having a marvelous experience of Pentecost. I would say, "Jesus, you couldn't expect me to do any more. Here I am teaching forty-seven first graders, going to prayer meetings, leading a youth group, and going to a prison to minister."

In the back of my mind I was really saying that I was going to play it safe. I wanted the respect and approval of people.

Then in June, the eve of Pentecost Sunday, in our convent in Tampa, I went into the chapel to make a Holy Hour for Pentecost. So, I sat there in our little oratory, saying "Jesus, here I am."

I had been in the chapel about five minutes when suddenly this extraordinary stillness descended on the chapel—it was like a cloud, like a fog. A voice said, "Briege." I turned to look toward the door because the voice was so clear it sounded as though someone had come into the chapel. No one was there, but I was very conscious that someone was present. The voice said to me as I turned back to the tabernacle, "You have my gift of healing. Go and use it."

As soon as I heard this, a burning sensation went through my body. I remember looking at my hands. It felt as though I had touched an electrical outlet. This burning sensation went through my hands and out of them. And then the stillness lifted.

I found myself kneeling, looking at the tabernacle, and saying, "Jesus, I don't want any gift of healing. Keep it for yourself." Then I made an act of contrition, not because I was sorry for what I had told Jesus, but for even thinking that Jesus would speak to me. Then I said to him, "Jesus, I'll make you a promise: I'll never tell anybody about this."

That Pentecost was very special to me since I had experienced the Holy Spirit and had learned to pray to him for all those gifts promised in Scripture and received in confirmation. All this was more important to me now.

I woke up on Pentecost morning and the voice was booming in my head, "You have my gift of healing: go and use it."

That day, at a prayer meeting at St. Joseph's Hospital in Tampa, I was tempted to tell a sister about what had happened the night before. But as I began to speak to her, I went blank.

Although nobody knew about this, I was invited to pray with a child. Years later, I found out that the child had been healed through that prayer.

In July and August, 1971, I went to study in Los Angeles, California. I went to prayer meetings there, but I never told anyone about the gift of healing. The Lord himself confirmed my gift of healing through two prophetic experiences.

One evening at a prayer meeting in St. Angela Merici Parish, I found myself sitting beside an Episcopalian priest, an elderly man. At the end of the meeting we all joined hands in prayer. After the prayer, he turned to me and said, "Sister, I've never spoken to a Roman Catholic nun before, but I have a message for you. As we were praying, I got this very strong feeling that you have the gift of healing—and you know you have it because the Lord spoke to you in your chapel in Florida."

I told the minister, "I really can't accept that. I belong to a strict congregation in Florida" and I went on to tell him all the reasons.

He just looked at me and said, "Tell me what happened in the chapel."

I said to myself, "How does he know? I never told one single person." I told him what had happened in the chapel, but said that I just couldn't accept it.

He looked at me and said, "Jesus will never force you. He reveals his will, but you are free to choose to follow him or not." Then he turned and walked away.

A few days later, in church after mass, I was talking with some people. A woman came up to me and said, "Sister, I don't know you, but when you went to communion, the Lord gave me a picture of you standing with a line of people coming to you. The Lord told me to tell you that you are being called into a great healing ministry."

In spite of the many people confirming what the Lord had said in our Tampa chapel, I still rejected his invitation to the ministry of healing.

Going to See the "Prophet"

During this time a group of ladies said they were going to see a "prophet." I got the notion that maybe he could help me. Maybe he would have a word for the future.

The prophet gave me a terrible, uneasy feeling. He looked at me and asked, "Are you married?" He must not know much about nuns, I thought. He asked me very unusual questions. I turned him off. He didn't tell me anything I didn't already know.

Two weeks later, a sister I knew came to town and I told her about my trip to the prophet. "I'd like to see him," she said. I should have had sense enough not to go back and to discourage my friend from going. However, I thought that while it had done me no good, maybe he would do her some good. I went with her.

Again, when he saw me, he asked, "Are you married?" I told him he must not be much of a prophet, that he didn't know anything about Catholic nuns, that I had given my life to Jesus.

He said to me, "You need your head cut off," and he traced his finger along the back of my neck around to the front. I joked about it and said, "Well, there's not much in it, but I'd have less without it."

He kept saying that I should not be a nun, that I should be doing something else with my young life. I kept arguing with him and he kept staring into my eyes. Within half an hour he had me in bits, completely confused. I was convinced people weren't good, that I could not help them. I was doubting my vocation and even doubting the existence of God; I had never before doubted either. I was convinced in that short time that I should get out of religious life. I came out crying in a terrible desolation. What I didn't realize was that I was in a confrontation with Satan.

When I came back to my own convent, the sister who was with me said it could not be of God, that I was too upset. She said that if it were of God, I would feel a deep peace.

I didn't tell any of the sisters about my turmoil and desire to leave the religious life because I thought it would upset them too much. I was alone, with no one to minister to me.

That night in bed I had a terrible confrontation with Satan. I couldn't sleep. I felt something choking me where the prophet had touched my neck. I couldn't cry out for help. It was like a force trying to get me to deny Christ and stop serving him. I couldn't pray. It was a terrible experience. Finally, I must have been able to call on Jesus, for the choking stopped. The next day, the sisters noticed I had a terrible color. I told them simply that I wasn't feeling well.

That day, we left on a short holiday to San Francisco. On the way, I kept saying, "God, please help me." At least I was calling on Jesus, but in the back of my mind was a feeling that I had to get out of religious life.

When I got to San Francisco, I stayed in my room. I took the Bible and said, "Jesus, I know this is your living Word. Please, I beg you, speak to me. Tell me especially about my vocation. Is this where I am supposed to be?"

I opened the Scriptures and the words were magnified, as though someone had put a magnifying glass over them. It was the passage from St. Paul, 1 Corinthians 7:32-35, about committing yourself to live the single life for the Lord. "I should like you to be free of all worries. The unmarried man is busy with the Lord's affairs, concerned with pleasing the Lord; but the married man is busy with this world's demands and occupied with pleasing his wife. This means he is divided. The virgin—indeed, any unmarried woman—is concerned with things of the Lord, in pursuit of holiness in body and spirit. The married woman, on the other hand, has the cares of this world to absorb her and is concerned with pleasing her husband. I am going into this with you for your own good. I have no desire to place restrictions on you, but I do want to promote what is good, what will help you to devote yourselves entirely to the Lord."

As I looked at those words in Scripture a marvelous peace and joy came down on me. From that moment I knew that what I had experienced was a deception and an attack of Satan. After that I sensed, however, that there was something more the Lord wanted to teach me.

I went to a charismatic conference in Anaheim, where Ralph Wilkerson, a very popular evangelist, spoke. I went up to meet him and he gave me a prophecy. He said, "Sister, your hands are anointed for the work of God."

I said to him, "I don't want to know anything about prophecy."

He interrupted me and said, "Sister, you went to the false prophet." He said that the "prophet" had destroyed many of the people of God, and had led many people out of the church. That was the first time anyone told me the man was a false prophet.

At the same conference, I talked to a Catholic priest and told him my story. He said to me, "Sister Briege, you don't need me to tell you anything else. You've had your answer in his living Word."

The Lord then led me back to the same Episcopalian priest who had told me I had the gift of healing.

At a prayer meeting in his home one night, I told him about this terrible experience. He said that someone had told him I was going to see the false prophet. He had wanted to stop me to protect me, but the Lord had told him not to intervene, that I had three lessons to learn from this, and that the Lord himself would protect me. He was led to pray for me while I went there and it was probably his prayers that saved me from the onslaught.

As he spoke to me, I realized I had indeed learned three lessons.

First, I should not have gone to a "prophet." I was trying to see the future. It was like fortune-telling, like seeking a false god. I was doing what God said not to do in the first commandment, "Thou shalt not put strange gods before me." My life must be centered in God; I must leave the future completely to him. He is the Way and I must abandon myself to him.

Second, I had to learn the difference between judging and discerning. The first time I went to the prophet, I knew something was wrong, but I thought I should not judge him. I had sensed the presence of evil, but I did not know what it was. I thought it might be my own attitude. I learned from this experience that I must pray for the gift of discernment.

Third, I learned that my vocation was not a gift from me to God, but that it was his gift to me. He had given me this vocation to liberate me for his gospel, not to bind me. I learned that I must get on my knees daily and thank the Lord for the gift.

A Fool for Jesus

On the plane back to Florida, I began thinking that it could not be mere coincidence that so many unrelated people all thought I had the gift of healing. I was praying the breviary and read the passage about the calming of the storm (Lk 8:22-25). It was as though the Lord said to me, "You know, I have complete control over the elements. They obey me. But you have a free will. You can choose." The Lord showed me he would never force me.

Then he gave me an image of a house. I have a great imagination, which I believe God uses to speak to me. In this image of the house, I was inside and a man came knocking at the door. I opened the door and he seemed to be a very nice man so I asked him in.

I told him, "See all these rooms. Make yourself at home, go anywhere you like in my house." I followed the man as he walked through all the rooms. There were many of them and they were very pretty. Suddenly he came upon a locked door. On the door in large dark type was PRIVATE PROPERTY—DO NOT ENTER. He turned to me, and as he turned, I recognized him to be Jesus. He asked me, "Briege, why can't I go in this room?"

I replied, "Come now, Jesus, look at all I've given you. I want to keep a little something for myself."

I heard him say, in this image, "You know, Briege, if you do not open that door, you will never know what it means to be truly free."

I remember looking at the image and saying to myself, "Now what is in that room?"

The Lord said, "I'll show you."

Inside that room was my reputation, what others thought of me. I didn't want Jesus in that room because I was preserving my good name and my reputation. I wanted to follow Jesus, but I wanted control of my life. I wasn't going to be a fool. Anything to do with the cross, with picking up my cross, that was out of the question.

I heard Jesus saying to me, "I thought you gave me your life."

Clearly the words of my vows came to me. I had promised to give my life to the Lord, for whatever he wanted from me in the Congregation of the Sisters of St. Clare. I saw myself kneeling before the mother general and the bishop and I heard myself saying those vows. At the same time, I heard Jesus say, as he pointed to the closed door, "On whose terms did you make that commitment?"

I realized that I had said, "Jesus, I love you and I give you my life—but on my terms." My religious life would never know fully the joy, the peace, the strength, and the courage—all that he wanted to give me—until I abandoned every part of my life and was willing to be a fool for him.

That day on the plane I said to him, "Jesus, you know I can't go back to Florida and tell people I have the gift of healing. I'll do the praying and you do the telling."

I came home to Florida, resumed teaching and going to prayer meetings and doing my regular duties. After two weeks, I went to a prayer meeting and was asked to share on my trip to California. I wasn't going to talk about healing, but as I got up, a lady jumped up and said, "Excuse me, Sister, I want to say something. You have the gift of healing. You know about it, but you are more worried about the approval of people than you are about God's will."

I looked at the woman and said, "I've never seen you in my life before. Who are you?"

She was a freelance writer from Canada. She said that when she woke up one morning, an image of my face appeared on her wall and she said, "It was revealed to me that God had given you the gift of healing but that you were afraid of it."

She did not know where I was, but had been led by the Holy Spirit to the Franciscan Center in Tampa where this very prayer meeting was being held. She told one of the sisters at the center, "I came here looking for the young Irish nun with the gift of healing." The nun said, "There was no Irish sister here." But the woman insisted, "She will be here."

I could not remember ever having seen this woman. I looked at her and said, "How do you know I'm Irish? Has the Holy Spirit told you?" I was making a joke of the whole thing.

She said, "I was in Orlando at a retreat you were on." She had been present when I was healed. She said to me, "You know God wants to use you in a ministry of healing." She kept talking, but I didn't hear anything else. I was in a panic and asking, "Oh, Lord! What's going to happen to my first graders? What am I going to do?"

And just as all these thoughts were coming into my mind, the most beautiful calmness descended upon me and this inner voice said, "Briege, why are you so worried? Do you believe in your vow of obedience? You know, I didn't give you the gift of vows to bind you, but I gave you the gift of vows to liberate you for my gospel. I was obedient to Mary and Joseph. I was obedient to my Father. What I ask of you is that you be obedient to your superiors and to those in authority in the church and I will work through them."

I said immediately, "Oh, thanks be to God, now it's my superior's problem!" That shows how one can use the vow of obedience to suit oneself. I was saying, "Well, now, I'll make this up in such a way that my superior and the principal will have to say no to my involvement in healing."

I said to my principal, "Sister, there's a woman who wants to write an article about me on the gift of healing in a magazine."

She looked at me and said, "Goodness, Briege! Have nothing to do with healing. It's too sensational."

That was exactly what I wanted to hear. "Don't worry, Sister. I'll not say a word about it to anybody."

I thought that if ever anybody asked me about the gift of healing, I'd just say I was under the vow of obedience and my superior doesn't wish me to talk about it.

Three weeks went by and all things were going along wonderfully. I was pretending to worry about the welfare of the congregation and the church, but I was really worried about Briege McKenna, about being a fool for Jesus, about being called a "faith healer." I didn't consider that Jesus was a faith healer.

Two weeks later, I got an invitation to speak to a women's guild in a parish. I was going to talk on prayer. I thought I did a good job. I talked a full hour on prayer and never once mentioned healing.

Two days later, I got a phone call from a woman who had been to the prayer meeting. She wanted to talk to me about healing. I was surprised because I had not mentioned healing, but I went to see her anyway. The woman told me her life story. It was very tragic. She had decided to kill herself, but circumstances would not permit it. Then she heard about my talk and became curious. When she saw and heard me, she found nothing right with me. She thought I was too young to know anything about prayer. She told me she got up and walked out. She didn't believe one word I was saying.

When she went home, she began again to contemplate suicide. That night she saw me walk into her room and stand beside her bed. My reaction was, "I didn't come to see you, I was at home in bed."

"Oh, no," she said, "you were here in my room last night. And I couldn't get rid of you." Apparently, the Lord used an image of me to reach this poor woman.

She told me that I said to her, "Why do you not believe in Jesus?" She said that whether her eyes were opened or closed she could see me and if she turned away from me there I was on the other side of the bed.

As she told me this, I thought, "Oh, Jesus, use me all you want during the day, but don't have me roaming through homes in the middle of the night."

And I heard Jesus say to me, "But I thought you said that if I'd do the telling you'd do the praying."

This woman had been in complete despair. Her face lit up and she said, "Do you think it's possible that God could help me?"

A short time later I got the flu. This same woman phoned me. She told me to put my trust in God, that he would take care of me. Only two weeks earlier, she had been contemplating suicide, and now she was ministering to me!

The Lord had really touched her life. She was completely converted, and came back into the Catholic church.

It was at that time that I said to myself, "Briege, mother superior or no mother superior, what you have to do is seek the Lord and do his will."

So, I went off to a priest, a good intellectual Scripture scholar. I didn't want to go to someone in the charismatic renewal for fear they would be too enthusiastic and would simply say something like, "Well, just follow the leading of the Spirit."

When I had told this priest my story, he said to me, "You know, if I was God I'd tell you to get lost. How many more times do you want Jesus to reveal his will? The only thing the Lord needs and asks of you is that just like Mary you say yes. God respects his children and he will only ask you to do his will. You have no power, so it has nothing to do with what you can do. What God is asking of you is whether you are willing to say yes and let him use you as his instrument."

I said, "But Father, how can I know when to pray? I can't just go up to someone who is sick and tell them I can pray for them for physical healing."

He smiled at me and said, "Sister, you don't have to tell people. If Jesus called you to this ministry of healing, then he will lead you to people and he will lead them to you. But, let's get this straight. Physical healing is only one facet of healing. There also are healings of emotions and memories. But the greatest healing is spiritual healing."

Then he took my hand and said, "Sister, go home to your community and live your community life. Do what you're called to do as a sister of St. Clare and if this call is from Jesus, he will open up the way."

Spiritual Healing

For the first six months after that, I was the skeptic. People were healed, but I still couldn't believe Jesus would work through me. I thought that I would have to be completely changed and perfect before he would use me. But the Lord still had more to teach me. I had to learn about what he considered the most serious sickness of all.

This lady stood up at a prayer meeting and said she wanted prayer for a woman who was both blind and paralyzed. My immediate reaction was, "Blind and paralyzed? That's too big a job for me, Lord." I was only starting out. I still didn't realize I was only the instrument. I felt the Lord saying I should go over to pray with the sick lady. I did.

When I went to see this woman I realized that sickness can do two things. It can make you a saint or you can become very bitter, depending on your attitude and disposition to prayer.

When I went in, this woman was very angry and had given up on God. When I put my hand on her, I said a little prayer with her and I felt the sensation of pins and needles, exactly as I had in the chapel when I had been given the gift of healing.

As I was praying, I was saying to myself, "Now Briege, don't go telling this woman she'll be healed. You know this is all psychological and she'll get disappointed. These tinglings in your hands are just your imagination."

I said the prayer with her, which at the time I thought was a harmless prayer and couldn't do much.

A few days later she sent for me. She said that she had been very skeptical of me. No nun had ever prayed like this and when I put my hands on her paralyzed arm, she thought I had stuck pins in her to make a good impression. She had felt something go through her arms. In the middle of the night, she got the power back into her arms. A few days later, she got her sight.

The woman's spiritual attitude totally changed. The Lord taught me that the inner healing, spiritual healing, was more important. If the spirit isn't healed, if a person is not brought closer to Jesus, what's the point? It's like the man who was lowered through the roof so Jesus could heal him (Mk 2:1-12). Jesus first said, "Your sins are forgiven." Then he healed him physically. It is more important to be healed of sin. That is the greatest sickness of all.

Home in Ireland

The next summer, 1972, I went to Ireland. The news about my ministry had reached there, although I never talked about the gift of healing, because I felt that what I did counted, not what I said. The father of a friend came up to me and said, "I don't believe in all that healing business, but a friend of mine is in the hospital and a prayer wouldn't hurt."

So I went to the hospital and prayed for a woman who was dying of cancer. The doctors had said there was no hope. On my way out, I noticed this poor man suffering from shingles and I prayed with him. The woman, a few days later, went home from the hospital in perfect health. When they came to examine her again, they could find nothing wrong with her. And the man with the shingles was healed, too.

The town was in an uproar looking for the healing nun. People were phoning and coming to see me. Every time they saw a nun in a brown habit, they would run after her.

My father said, "You know, you pray enough in America. I thought you were here on holiday." People were shouting and whistling at my father as he worked in the fields, asking him where they could find Sister Briege. He said to me, "My, Briege, you have a lot of friends."

I spent a lot of time with my Auntie Lizzie, and sometimes there were as many as sixty cars parked outside her house. When I was home she couldn't get any work done with all those people coming around looking for me and telling her all their sicknesses. Auntie Lizzie would often say, "Me head's busting from all these sicknesses."

Shortly after the healing of the woman with cancer and the man with shingles, I was praying in the cathedral in Newry. I had many concerns: was I calling attention to myself, with all those people talking about me and looking for me? People were saying to me, "Be careful because you could really get yourself into trouble. You know the bishop doesn't know anything about it. What are you going to do?"

So I sat in the cathedral and I said, "Look, Jesus, I'm home on my holidays; is this your will that I should be doing this? I don't want to do anything against your will." Then I asked him to teach me how to pray for people.

As I prayed, an old man came into the church. He knelt down on the opposite side of the church. After a while, he shouted out to me, "Sister would you pray for me?" He held up his arm and said, "I fell off my bicycle and hurt my wrist."

I called him over and asked him, "Have you heard of me?"

He said, "No, I just noticed you were a nun and thought you might say a prayer for me."

I prayed for him and he promised to say a decade of the rosary for me. He went back to his place in front of the statue of our Lady. I could hear him praying the rosary. In the middle of the decade he looked over and said, "God, that was a powerful prayer. Could you write it out? The pain and the swelling are all gone."

I heard the Lord say, "You see, I brought in a man off the street. That's why I brought you home, to touch my people." That answered my first question.

Next, the Lord showed me a picture of an enormous pink telephone over the tabernacle. I thought it was a distraction and I wanted to get it out of my mind. But there were these words in dark print under the telephone: "The telephone is a means of communication. People talk to each other on it. I can also use it. You use the phone. People will hear you but experience me." It was then that he told me to pray over the phone with people, that I didn't have to see them, that all I had to do was unite with them before Jesus. He is not limited by time and space. That answered my second question.

When I went back to the motherhouse, a sister said that a man from England wanted to come see me for prayer. He had a severe skin problem. I told the sister, "He doesn't have to come here, I'll pray for him by phone."

She looked at me and said, "Does it work that way, too?"

I said, "I don't know but we'll have a go."

When the man phoned me and I prayed with him, he was completely healed.

While in Ireland, one of the sisters from the school said that a lady who worked there had a daughter in the hospital with a serious skin problem. I couldn't go there, but I asked her to send the mother to me. I prayed with the mother and within a few days, the girl had been totally healed and had skin like a new baby.

I think the Lord allowed me to see and experience these physical healings not so much for the people as for me.

Jesus Is the Teacher

Mother Angelica from Birmingham, Alabama, the Franciscan nun who founded the first Catholic satellite television network, is widely known for her wit and wisdom. I had given a retreat to priests in Birmingham with Fr. Harold Cohen from New Orleans. Mother had heard about me and invited me to her monastery to make a retreat.

I thought that this would be a good time to learn more about healing, so I arrived with all kinds of books on healing written by recognized experts. I thought I'd learn from them why people aren't healed, and then when they ask me, I'd be able to give them an answer off the tip of my tongue.

On the first day, I read the first chapter of a book, and the next morning I couldn't remember anything. For several days, I couldn't remember anything I'd read.

Finally, one day, Mother Angelica took me by the hand and brought me into the chapel. She pointed up at the monstrance where the Eucharist was exposed and she said to me, "If Jesus wanted you to be somebody else, he would have made you somebody else. He made you to be Briege McKenna—and," she said, still pointing to the Lord, "there's the teacher. Don't be trying to copy other people's styles. Come to Jesus and let him teach you."

That day I made a commitment to spend two or three hours a day in personal prayer. Then the Lord started to teach me that I didn't have to answer all the questions. Not everybody was going to be healed physically, but that wasn't my business. My business was not to defend him, but to proclaim him.

TWO

The Lord Lives in a Battered Tent

Taking Mother Angelica's advice, I made my commitment to spend two to three hours daily before the Blessed Sacrament.

St. Clare, the foundress of our congregation of sisters, is always depicted in statues and pictures holding up the Blessed Sacrament in a monstrance. The story is told that when enemies attacked Assisi, where she lived, Clare held up the monstrance and the power of her faith in her Lord drove them back. The Eucharist is historically at the center of our life at the Congregation of the Sisters of St. Clare.

I made the commitment that wherever I went, in every country, I would spend three hours before the Lord. This is the only request I have always made of bishops and priests throughout the world—that they house me in a convent or some place where the Blessed Sacrament is available and that they arrange my schedule so that I can have my prayer time.

I find it amazing how, when I have not been able to go to a convent, the Lord has made sure that wherever I was, there was within a few blocks a place where I could adore the Blessed Sacrament. If we make that commitment to prayer, he will not be outdone in generosity.

Sometimes, however, I have found it difficult to get people to realize that I really need the full three hours in prayer. It is easy for people to find good reasons for me to give up my prayer time. They can point to people who need ministry.

I've had to remind myself continually that I need Jesus more than those people need me. If I didn't go to Jesus in prayer, I would have nothing to offer them. I don't pray because I am holy, but because I want to become holy and I need Jesus to teach me.

The discipline of sitting before the Lord is very important. It is only when your spirit is still and when the ears of your spirit are open that you can really hear the Lord and experience the wisdom and insights that come from the Holy Spirit.

It was difficult to believe in the beginning that Jesus would speak to me and teach me in those hours of prayer, but there are many lessons I learned from the Lord through prayer that have changed my life as well as the lives of others to whom I ministered.

Keeping the Commitment to Prayer

Late one evening, during the Intercession for Priests in Dublin, Ireland, Fr. Kevin Scallon asked me to minister during the priests' prayer time, which I used myself as one of my hours of prayer. There was, actually, a great need for my ministry at the Intercession. I didn't want to refuse this request, which seemed reasonable enough, but at the same time I was torn about giving up this hour of prayer.

I told him I would make myself available during this time. Before going to bed, late that night, I put up a notice on the bulletin board advising the priests that I would be able to see them by appointment while everyone else was in the chapel praying before the Blessed Sacrament.

Nobody knew but myself and Father Kevin that I had decided to give up this hour of prayer to minister. But the very next morning, an elderly priest came up to me in the corridor and said, "Sister Briege, I know you pray, but I have something to tell you and I don't know how to tell you." He had trouble getting to the point and I kept wondering what he was going to tell me. Finally, he told me that the night before he couldn't sleep because as he went to bed he heard an inner voice saying, "Go to Sister Briege and tell her that the hour she gave away is my hour and I want that hour for myself."

After he said this, he looked at me and smiled and said, "It doesn't make much sense, does it?"

Little did he know how much sense it made to me. I thanked him. It was at that moment that I realized how much Jesus wanted me to hold to my commitment, not because he needed me but because he wanted to love me and teach me. We forget, sometimes, that Jesus is a living person who waits for us. Here he was waiting for me.

This was a great lesson for me. I am not committing those three hours to a project but to a living person, and that living person is Jesus who is always there. He is there not for what I can give him but for what he can give to me.

I went to Father Kevin and told him about the old priest. He immediately told me to cancel the plans and return to my original schedule.

Then I went into the chapel where everyone else was adoring the Blessed Sacrament and praying. I sat down, feeling a little guilty that the Lord had had to remind me of my commitment.

As I closed my eyes, the Lord gave me an image of a monastery. There was a wall around the monastery and a door. I went through the door. Then I came to another door which had a sign on it: "Enclosure."

I looked at this door and the Lord said to me, "You see, Briege, this door has 'Enclosure' on it. You cannot go in there. The people in there don't come out because they have made a commitment to live their lives enclosed from the world."

"This is only to remind you," the Lord said, "that these are only physical walls and this is not what makes a contemplative. What makes a contemplative is the enclosure in the heart."

It was then that the Lord revealed to me that, even though I am not a cloistered nun, I must have a contemplative spirit. I must be a woman who at special times can close that cloister of the heart and let no one else in, that the special times are for the Lord alone. Before I make commitments to other people I must ask myself if I have kept my commitment to Jesus.

I became more aware of the need to be faithful in prayer. Prayer is a gift of God. To cooperate with the gift, I have to have the discipline to give time to prayer. I learned that if I am willing to give the time to prayer, then God will give me grace and teach me how to pray. He will change me through prayer.

What Happens in Prayer

It is not easy to sit before the Lord. Sometimes a person can feel bored or without anything to say. A person can be distracted by many serious matters. It is easy to say, "Oh, what's the use?" or "What good is this doing me? I don't feel a thing!"

Nothing may seem to be happening while you are at prayer, but the proof of the power of prayer comes later, when you are working or ministering. You realize the inner strength that prayer has given you—as well as the insights and wisdom that you receive later when they are needed.

When I mention that I spend three hours in prayer each day, people sometimes say, "Where do you get the time?" or "What do you say for three hours? I'd get bored." Some people have said, "I couldn't even pray for half an hour!"

The Lord asked me for three hours; he doesn't ask it of everybody. For a lay person or a priest or a sister working at a full-time job, three hours may be impossible and even undesirable. Whether you're a priest or sister, or a lay person or a deacon, you must find some time to pray. I think those of us who are committed in the church should give the Lord no less than an hour in prayer. But each of us has to find the time that is suitable for his or her own vocation.

I feel very privileged that, being a sister and living in a convent, I have the Blessed Sacrament in my home. I can go to the Lord at any time. But I encourage everyone to have a special place, a corner or a room, that is reserved for prayer. This special place, with an icon or image of Jesus, will help you leave for a moment the cares of the world and draw you into close communion with the Lord.

One thing the Lord has done for me through this discipline of prayer is to give me a great teaching on healing. He has shown me how different Scriptures relate to what he was teaching—for he always taught when he healed. He has shown me how his teaching and the Scriptures relate to my ministry in the present day.

I'd like to share a teaching that came to me one day as I sat before the Lord. I was just looking at the Blessed Sacrament and adoring Jesus and telling him I didn't have much to say except that I loved him.

I felt as though the Lord said to me, "Well, don't you know that you don't have to say anything to me? Just be with me. Come into my presence. It's not what you do for me, it's what I want to do for you."

Then I got an image of a person going out of his house and sitting in the sun. As he sat in the sun, he didn't do a thing, but he started to change color. People who saw him knew he had been in the sun because his skin showed it. The man knew it, too, because he felt the effects of the sun: the warmth and the light.

I heard the Lord saying, "So it is when you come into my presence. You will experience the effects of your time spent with me. People will see it in your actions."

It was a great teaching to me, knowing that I didn't always have to be saying things but all I had to do was be there with Jesus.

Prayer and Holiness

Prayer keeps us in touch with Jesus. It makes us aware of what is holy. Prayer helps us discern what comes from God. Prayer also makes us sensitive to what is not holy, to what does not come from God.

My own personal prayer time gave me a new awareness of how sin is growing in the world. It has also made me aware that I can overlook the sins and imperfections in my own life while I see all the sin in the world.

I went to New Orleans for a five-day retreat. One night, I woke up with a start. As I woke up, I looked up at the ceiling and there, as though on a movie or television screen, was a picture of a beautiful garden. The garden had many flowers and among these flowers were little weeds.

The Lord said to me, "Briege, this is your soul." The flowers represented the virtues I was trying to cultivate in my efforts to become holy. But at the same time, as I walked around the garden admiring the flowers, I was looking at the weeds and saying, "Oh, they're just small and they won't do a bit of harm." I saw myself giving the weeds a little pat saying, "I'll not bother with you. You're just little weeds."

Then the Lord said to me, "Those weeds represent sin. You are comparing yourself with the world, with all the evil in the world."

You know how it is. We hear about all the terrible things that go on in the world and then we say, "Oh, but I don't kill or steal. I don't push drugs. I don't sell my body in prostitution," and so on.

The Lord said to me, "You are not called to compare yourself with the world. You are called to compare yourself with me. I am your model. Not the world. You must never accept sin."

I realized I was falling into the very trap I was preaching about. I was not being vigilant about the sin in my life.

As I continued to look at the image, I saw the gardener coming in. He looked at me and said, "If you let me, I'll eradicate those weeds for you. Then the flowers will have a brighter color and there will be greater growth in your garden."

The greatest sickness today is not sickness of the body but of the soul. The sickness of the soul can only be healed by the divine physician. The Lord showed me that the sacrament of reconciliation was the means he used to eradicate sin, that this is a great sacrament to help us grow in holiness. In this sacrament, the living Jesus comes to fight the enemy of your soul.

The Lord showed me two other things through this image. First, I cannot save myself. I cannot make my garden beautiful on my own; I cannot become holy on my own. I must acknowledge that I am a sinner. If I don't I am self-righteous and proud.

Second, I learned the value of repentance and the beauty of confession. Confession is coming to the Jesus who loves me. He wants me to reflect his beauty and love. He wants me to understand that his love for me led to his suffering and death.

Fr. Frank Sullivan, a professor of theology at the Gregorian University in Rome, once said, "If you want to know what God thought of sin, read the passion of Jesus." The passion of Jesus shows what God thinks of sin, how despicable he finds it.

In the passion of Jesus we see also the great love of Jesus for his Father and for us. We see how much he loves us, that he is willing to suffer and die in our place.

As a result of this insight from the Lord, I found myself kneeling by my bed. I made a commitment to the Lord that I would try to go to confession every two weeks.

When I share this with people, they sometimes ask me, "What do you tell the priest? I wouldn't know what to say to him." I always say to them, "Ask whoever you're living with and they will tell you your sins!"

The Beauty of Confession

Going to confession regularly has given me a new appreciation for this sacrament. I often ask why people don't go to confession today more than they do. It can't be that we're sinning less. Can we have lost our appreciation for the sacrament of reconciliation because we no longer realize how terrible sin is? Is it that we no longer appreciate the suffering and death of Jesus, that he died for us? Do we no longer realize that all we have to do, to claim the benefits of his suffering, is to confess our sins and to rely on his mercy?

It is much easier to strive for holiness when you can go to Jesus in this sacrament regularly. It is a great spiritual consolation, and a reminder of Jesus' great love, to be able to come to the priest and to hear those great words, "Your sins are forgiven." As long as we are making an effort to avoid sin, we know that in the sacrament of reconciliation we are cleansed and we can start afresh.

I'm often reminded, thinking of how we struggle with sin, of Jesus on his way to Calvary. He fell often, but he always got up again. That's what our call is, to strive continuously for holiness.

Striving for holiness means admitting that although I am weak and I am going to sin again, I have to get up and keep going. As a Catholic, there is no greater way for me to declare my desire for holiness than to come to Jesus asking him to forgive me and give me the grace to keep going.

Because of this frequent celebration of the sacrament of reconciliation, the Lord has led people to me. They come to me to talk about their inner life, about moral problems that they have.

One time, when I was traveling on a plane, the steward came up to me and asked me if he could speak with me. I'll call him Arthur, although that is not his real name.

Arthur told me he was a Catholic and that he went to mass every Sunday, but that he had a very serious moral problem. He was afraid to go to confession. He hadn't been in ten years. He was afraid to talk to a priest because ten years before he had had a bad experience in confession.

He went into great detail with me about his problem. By this time he was crying. He said, "Sister, I don't know what to do. I'm scared. I know I'm going to hell. I do everything I can to make up for what I am doing wrong, but I don't seem to be able to overcome it."

I looked at him and said, "You know, Arthur, you don't have to go into a box to go to confession." I told him about the new rite of reconciliation and what I understood about the sacrament.

He said, "But I don't know how to go to confession. I haven't been there in years."

I told him, "Well, you've gone to confession to me, but I am not a priest and can't give you absolution. But what you told me, you should go and tell a priest."

He said, "Is that how you go to confession?" This made me realize that many people don't go to confession simply because they have forgotten how and not because they don't want to go. Because of the many changes in the Catholic church, people feel that the priest will think poorly of them if they go for forgiveness and don't even know how to go about it.

I took Arthur's hand and said, "I'm going to say a prayer for you and ask Jesus to give you the courage. And then I'll arrange for a priest to see you."

As I began to pray with him, the Lord gave me two images that, for my own life as well as for Arthur's, were very revealing.

In the first image, I saw Arthur caught in a net, as though someone had thrown it over him and secured him in it. Then I saw a man come up to him and open the net and let him out of it. The net represented sin; the man who opened the net was the priest whom God uses to give us tangible proof of forgiveness and healing.

In the second image, I saw a man near an iceberg. He had a small icepick. He kept picking away at the iceberg and he finally got it down just below the water, and he was very satisfied. At least he had done that much. He went off, but when he turned around and looked back, the iceberg was up again.

The Lord showed me that Arthur was doing things to make reparation to God for sin. He was trying to prove to God that he loved him and that he really was sincere by doing all kinds of good works. Arthur was trying to sanctify himself and to overcome his own sinfulness without the help of God.

Arthur found it hard to accept that Jesus would forgive him. He could not understand that Jesus came to save sinners, not the righteous.

I explained to him that the sacrament of reconciliation is not just for wiping away the sins already committed, but that the grace of the sacrament enables people to eradicate the sinful habit in their lives.

I realized as I spoke with Arthur that the more I went to the sacrament, the less I fell into my own sins. The sacrament gave me hope in the Lord's mercy and strength in the face of temptation.

Arthur, there and then on the plane, made a commitment. He said, "Sister, you find a priest and I will go to confession." After ten years he went to confession. The priest was compassionate and able to lead him into true repentance and a real conversion experience.

Three months later, I talked to that young man. He told me that he was now going to confession almost every week. And he said, "You know, Sister, I still get the temptations, but I've never fallen back into that sin again. God has taught me that temptation is not a sin and that I can come back to him and I get the strength to overcome sin. I thank you for teaching me that Jesus is not a harsh judge, but compassionate and waiting to put his arms about me and receive me back like the prodigal son."

In speaking of sin, repentance, and spiritual growth, we must realize that the Evil One has a very subtle weapon he uses to discourage souls in their quest for God. That weapon is guilt.

There is such a thing as healthy guilt. When we have done something wrong and we feel guilty, that is our conscience talking to us. That's how we know we must confess and repent.

But some people have a terrible guilt hanging over their heads even after they have been to confession. This robs them of the joy of the Lord and of receiving the Lord's forgiveness in a personal and conscious way. Not to be able to forgive yourself is pride.

When we go to confession, we realize that we fell, but Jesus forgives us. That's the beauty of our good and compassionate God. As St. Paul says, "He died for us while we were still in sin" (Rm 5:8). That means he loves us even when we are in sin.

One of my favorite stories in Scripture is about Peter saying to Jesus, "I'll never deny you. I'll never leave you" (Mk 14:29-31). Jesus who knows us so well was able to say to him, "Before the cock crows twice, you will have denied me three times."

It is true that Peter denied the Lord, but when the Lord looked at him, he repented and wept bitterly for his sin (Mk 14:72).

But Peter forgave himself. If he hadn't, he couldn't have taken on the task the Lord gave him to lead his brothers and to encourage them. The difference between Peter and Judas was Peter's ability to say, "Well, I sinned and denied my Master, but he has forgiven me." Judas couldn't forgive himself and couldn't accept God's forgiveness.

We must not allow guilt to beat us to the ground. It must not lead us into discouragement or depression. We have to keep humbling ourselves and saying, "Jesus, I did it again; please forgive me" and then to get up and keep going.

What to Do in Prayer

Part of the getting up and going is your commitment to prayer. Prayer is disciplined. It is not haphazard. To some degree it is organized. I'd like to share how I spend my three hours in prayer and how the Lord has helped me to grow in my prayer life.

When I go into the chapel, I first spend time praising God. I pray in tongues and praise the Lord. I thank the Lord for being the Lord.

Jesus said, "If my people don't praise me the stones will cry out" (Lk 19:40). If you ever find it hard to praise the Lord, just take up the psalms, because they are full of praise.

I find in my own prayer time that praise brings me out of the distractions of my everyday life and helps me to open up to the Spirit. We're not like a radio. We can't just switch off what we were doing and all of a sudden find ourselves absorbed in God. You carry with you what you've been doing in the daytime and the events and happenings in your life. When you bring them to prayer, the only way to keep them from becoming a distraction is to submit them to the Lord in a spirit of praise.

I also read Scripture. I believe that everything that is written in the word of God has a message for each of us, especially the readings from daily mass.

No matter the time, somewhere in the world on that day those Scriptures are being proclaimed. I often think that somewhere, some person is being converted by that gospel.

There is no greater way, I feel, to come into union with the mind and the spirit of the church than by reading these daily Scriptures. I read and reread them many times and then I try to put myself into those Scriptures to find out what they may be saying to me.

I also pray the rosary. I'm known for being fast at praying the rosary in a group, but in my prayer time, I try to pray it slowly and meditate on its mysteries.

Then I just sit there and I talk with Jesus. The first thing a person does when speaking to another person is to look at him. If someone says "hello" to you, you look at that person. If that person continues to speak to you, you continue looking at him.

St. Teresa, in speaking of recognizing the Lord's presence, said, "The failure to realize that Someone is there, that God is there, lies in the root of all our problems in prayer. We will not do with him what we expect others to do with us when they speak to us—to look at him."

We have difficulty picturing Jesus really present to us. This is the reason St. Teresa speaks of the value of sacred images, statues, and icons—or especially, for us Catholics, the Eucharist which helps us focus on the real, tangible presence of Jesus.

I have a beautiful picture of the holy face of Jesus and I often use it to talk to him. The interesting thing is that if you start talking to him and you learn to listen, then he starts talking back to you. This is St. Teresa's sovereign way to prayer: "Only look at him."

She said, "Before beginning to pray and while praying, let your interior glance rest on the One who is there and should you be distracted, renew your glance. Keep reminding yourself that Jesus is looking at you and you are looking at him."

Ultimately, no one can teach you how to pray except Jesus. The lack of instruction is not the problem. There are many books which help and guide us in prayer. But the problem is making the time for prayer, making oneself available to go and sit with Jesus.

Look at Jesus and the apostles. He didn't just give them a teaching; he brought them with him, spent time with them. Prayer really starts off with spending time with the Lord.

The Battered Tent

As a young sister, I often heard talks about living in the presence of God. In today's society, because of so much noise and the difficulty of finding places of silence, people say they find it difficult to be aware of Jesus.

Some years ago, on my annual retreat, I found myself under terrible temptations and discouragement. Every temptation you can think of, I had that night. On my way to mass the next morning, I felt very battered and discouraged because of the attacks and temptations of the preceding night.

As I walked up to communion, I made an act of faith. I said, "Jesus, I know I am receiving you, but I feel so discouraged, so downhearted, and so unworthy to receive you."

This was the way I felt as I received communion. As I received the sacred Host and turned to go back to my place, I received a clear image of a tent. I remember looking at the tent and thinking, "Well, that poor tent is really battered." I remember examining it and saying, "It must have gone through a terrible storm."

As I got to my pew and knelt down, I saw a man coming to go into the tent. I saw myself in the image and I was telling the man, "Oh, you can't go in there, it's a mess. It's all battered. There are big holes in it."

The man looked at me and smiled and said, "What do you mean? I live in here."

At that moment, I realized that I was the battered tent, that I had been battered with the temptations to sin and discouragement and all those things that had harassed me during the night. Now, Jesus was showing me that, battered and all, he still made his home in me—and that he had just come to me again under the appearance of the sacred Host.

It was very humbling: I had never before thought of myself as an old battered tent! Then it was as if Jesus took me into the tent. I saw him sitting at this table and I was sitting there with him. He took hold of my two hands and talked to me across this table.

As he talked to me, I was eyeing this tent and saying, "Oh, my God, look at this tent! What will people think? Look at this messy tent!"

I excused myself and took my hands out of Jesus' hands. I pulled out the chair and got on it and began fixing the holes in the tent. I was thinking, "What will people say if they see these holes?" I got very busy about making the tent look good for other people.

It was then that I felt Jesus gently pull me down. He looked at me, with great kindness and he said, "Briege, if you become preoccupied with these holes and your work in fixing these holes, then you'll forget about me. But if you become preoccupied with me, then I'll fix your tent."

I realized that I was spending too much time worrying about the temptations and my sins, about how I was going to cope and about what other people thought. The Lord showed me that conversion and repentance happen when we become preoccupied with Jesus and turn to him. When you turn to

Jesus, you automatically turn away from sin. You cannot give your full attention to Jesus and at the same time turn to sin.

That's what happened to all the great saints in the church: they turned to Jesus and away from sin. Look at St. Francis of Assisi. He became totally preoccupied with Jesus and forgot all about the things he wanted to do in his life and all the things that were wrong in his life. God took care of them. The same is true for St. Paul, St. Peter, St. Ignatius, St. Mary Magdalen, and St. Thomas Aquinas, to name only a few.

We all must remember that when we sin, we must not become preoccupied with the sin and keep going back over the sin, but turn to Jesus. When you begin to try to please him and to live for him, then he changes your life.

The Lord showed me this second lesson using the tent. Again, I was seated at the table with him. I peeped out of the tent and saw people with many problems, sicknesses, and difficulties coming toward the tent. I said, "Oh, I've got to go because all these people need me." I jumped up and said, "Oh, God, how am I going to deal with all these problems, so many people and so many problems?"

As I was standing at the doorway of the tent trying to figure out how I was going to help them, I again felt Jesus' hand pull me back. He shook his finger and with a little smile he said, "They are not coming to you for you to solve their problems. They are only coming to you because I live in you. If you get up and say, 'I have to do it,' then you'll forget that I'm the healer and I'm the one who brings peace. I'm the one who heals the sick. All I need is for you to be the instrument. So you just sit down now and let me go to the door."

I found myself smiling as I said to Jesus, "Yes, now I know why you said that when someone trusts you there is no failure. If I try to do it myself, I fail."

From that experience, I became more conscious that it is Jesus who has the power and who accomplishes all the work. As St. Paul says, "It is not I who live, but Christ lives in me" (Gal

2:20). Often, when I get invitations to go throughout the world speaking to all kinds of people—bishops, priests, doctors—I get the feeling, "I couldn't do that." And I hear Jesus saying, "No you can't, but I can. Let me do it through you."

It's true. I can't do it. The day I believe I can, I have run off and left him sitting there at the table in that battered tent.

The day I start trying to do it myself is the day I will get frustrated and make mistakes. It is the day Briege starts building her own kingdom instead of the Lord's.

THREE

The Lord Is the Healer

J ESUS IS THE HEALER. He has a "way" of healing, which is found
in Scripture. Each healing Jesus performed was tied in with
a teaching. He didn't heal and just leave it there. With each
opportunity, he would teach his disciples.

As I walked daily with the Lord in prayer, he began to teach
me more and more about his healing ministry. He enabled me
to be more effective in letting him work through me.

In the very beginning of the healing ministry, there were
many things I didn't understand. One of the questions many
people asked me—and that I asked myself—was, "What
happens when you pray for people and they do not get well,
when they die, when the Lord answers prayer by taking a person
home? How do you comfort the loved ones in this shattering
experience when they had hoped and prayed for a healing?"

It was through an experience like this that I learned one
definition of healing. Today I use this definition when people
ask me what the healing ministry is all about.

Saying Yes to God

Some years ago, a father of a little nine-year-old girl came to
see me. He was very distraught. This was their only child and
she was dying of leukemia. He had heard that I had been used as

the Lord's instrument to bring the Lord's healing to people with leukemia, especially children.

In desperation he said, "I've tried everything and nothing worked. I even tried Jesus and he didn't work, so now it's up to you."

I replied, "If you forget that I only work for Jesus, that I'm only his instrument, you'll again be very disappointed."

I went to the hospital with him, hoping that I would at least be able to console him. At the hospital, the little girl was lying there in great suffering and dying. As I knelt down and took the child's hand it was as if through that little hand, I felt transmitted to me the message, "I don't need healing, but my dad needs healing. I'm happy to go."

I decided I had to talk to the father, because he was trying to pressure me into saying his daughter was going to be healed. That's what he really wanted to hear. If Sister Briege said that, it would make him feel good.

As I knelt at that bedside, I wanted to be able to say, "She's going to be healed the way you want." But then I would be taking God's place. I would be putting myself in a position in which I allowed sympathy to speak for me. Sympathy is good, but it mustn't take on the role of speaking for God.

I went out of the ward with the father into the waiting room and spoke with him and his wife. I took their hands and said, "I'd love to tell you that Mary is going to be healed the way you want, but I don't know how she is going to be healed. But I know that Jesus will not disappoint you because he loves you and he loves your little Mary a lot more than anybody. He will give you the strength you need and he will heal Mary the way that he knows best."

At the time when I was talking to the parents, they could not accept what I was saying. They were very upset. As I left the hospital I wanted to be able to heal Mary, but realized I could not. This realization, that you can't do what you want to do, shows that you are only an instrument, that you have no control over what God does.

People often act as though you can manipulate God into doing what you want him to do. If you believe enough or say the right things or if you have enough faith, then God has to work. But through this experience God taught me that he doesn't change to suit us. In the process of praying and through prayer we change to fit into God's will.

When we realize this, we can accept difficult situations because God supplies the strength, grace, and vision. He shows us his will with more clarity.

About three days after my visit to the hospital, the parents phoned to tell me that little Mary had died. Immediately I thought, "I'd better go to see them. They must be very heartbroken."

I'll always remember seeing the beautiful little girl in the coffin, at the funeral home and the parents standing there. The father came to me and embraced me and said, "Sister Briege, I want to thank you." He turned around, stretched his hand toward his little girl, and he said, "You know, I now realize that healing doesn't mean getting my own way, but getting the strength and the grace to say yes to God's way. I realize now that little Mary wasn't mine. She was given to me to nurture and to love and to care for, but she was the Lord's—and who am I to tell God what he should do?

"But," he said, "I want to tell you that two days ago I couldn't have accepted this. An hour before she died, I couldn't have accepted it. Now I understand that God doesn't give us strength for something that we're going to have to face a month from now or two weeks from now. He gives us the strength at the moment we need the strength. I just want to thank you. Mary was healed and brought to heaven, but I, her dad, was left to tell of the beauty of the Lord's strength and that he answers prayer."

What that father said tells us what healing is all about. Healing is saying yes to God. When we, as the Lord's children, can say yes to him, we will never be hurt. The Lord never does anything in our lives that will hurt us. He is a God of love. It is in our resistance and our pulling away and saying no that we actually hurt ourselves.

I see that my mission in this healing ministry is to help people in all walks of life to say yes to God, just as I must say yes to God in my own daily life.

Let's look at some gospel stories to see how Jesus healed during his ministry on earth, and how people were involved with Jesus as he healed. This reflection will help us understand better how he heals today. He is the same God now as he was then and we are not that different from the people who lived in New Testament times.

The Paralytic

Jesus was speaking to a house filled with people. There were so many people, they overflowed into the yard. They had come to listen to Jesus who had become known as a great healer.

Some men had a friend who was a paralytic. Of course, like any good friends, when they heard there was someone who could heal the paralytic, they decided to bring him to Jesus. Since he couldn't walk, they carried him. If you really love someone, you bring him to Jesus.

When they got there, the Gospel tells us, there were so many people they could not get in. But they persevered. They climbed up on the roof, removed some tiles and lowered the man to the floor before Jesus.

Jesus could see this man was paralyzed. He could see the withered legs. That was why his friends brought him. They didn't bring him for any other reason but to get those withered legs healed.

But as Jesus looked at him, he looked beyond the withered legs. He looked at what was most important. The greatest paralysis is that of the soul which is caused by sin. Jesus looked at the man's soul and he said to him, "Your sins are forgiven."

People started whispering and saying, "What authority has he to forgive sins?" and "Who is he to speak like this?"

Through reflection on this gospel story, the Lord taught me

there is need for order and priority in our lives. What is more important: physical healing of withered legs or spiritual healing?

For us, it is much more important to seek after healing of the soul. You know, millions of dollars are spent on research to heal the body. That is good. The Lord wants us to use resources to find cures. Yet it seems that we don't have equal zeal getting rid of sin which causes sickness of the soul.

Many people come to me for physical healing and they have no interest in spiritual healing. Once a man phoned me and told me he had a very bad leg. I responded, "I'll pray with you for spiritual healing and physical healing as well."

He said, "Oh, no, that's all right. Don't bother about the spiritual healing. It's just my leg that needs healing."

I said to him, "You'll not need your leg to get into heaven, but you'll sure need a healthy soul."

People aren't always aware of their need for spiritual healing. This poses a danger for people in the healing ministry. We can become too preoccupied and too excited with physical healings which should be a sign that leads to spiritual healing and a deeper relationship with Jesus.

One time, when I was teaching school, a gentleman came to my classroom. He said to me, "Sister, my wife is all the time after me to go and see Sister Briege and get her to pray with me because she has the gift of healing and she can help me. But, Sister Briege, I don't believe in you. I told my wife, 'I don't really believe that Sister Briege has the gift of healing. I think she's a fake. I don't believe in her at all.'"

His wife said, "Go anyway. She'll help you."

He repeated that he didn't believe in me.

I remember thinking, what great courage he has to be so honest! I said to him, "You don't have to believe in me. It's not written in the Bible that you have to believe in Briege McKenna. But do you believe in Jesus?"

He looked surprised and he said, "Of course, I believe in Jesus."

"That's all you need. I can pray with you. You don't have to believe in me, but you believe that Jesus can heal you."

Then I asked him, "What do you want to be healed of?"

He said, "Well, that's another thing. I said to my wife that it's rather a strange thing to be asking a nun to pray for. But my work is outdoors and it's very hot to be working outdoors here in Florida. I would love to be able to drink a beer to cool me down. I love beer but I have a bad stomach and it doesn't agree with me. I'd like you to pray that I could take one or two beers to cool me down."

I remember thinking as he told me this, "What a lame kind of need! And yet, it's important to him."

So I prayed with him and while praying I became amused. I thought, "I've been praying with a lot of alcoholics to stop drinking and here I am praying for this man so that he can start!"

I could see, as I was praying with him, that somehow he was moved by the prayer. Some time later, I learned from his wife and from the man himself that he had had a very serious moral problem, although he did not tell me what it was. The need he had had in his life was really much greater than this trivial thing about drinking beer.

The man was totally converted to the Lord and had a marvelous inner healing of his spiritual life. He became a man of deep commitment to the Lord. Just as Jesus did for the paralytic, he healed this man both physically and spiritually.

In my own healing, I went to the Lord looking for spiritual help because that is really what I was crying out for. My legs, like the paralytic's, were deformed, but it was my soul that I was most concerned with. There, too, the Lord taught me a beautiful lesson. You don't have to separate the spiritual from the physical.

I was not asking for a physical healing because I thought the soul was much more important. The Lord showed me I can ask him for everything. I also learned that many of our sicknesses can be rooted in the sickness of our soul.

The Centurion's Servant (Matthew 8:5-13)

A centurion came to Jesus to beg for the healing of his servant boy. Jesus said, "I'll come right away." Immediately the centurion said, "Oh, no. You don't have to come. I'm not worthy to have you under my roof. Just give an order and I believe my servant boy will be healed."

I find two teachings in this passage. One is healing from a distance. Sometimes, people believe that one who prays for healing has to be with the sick person. They will say, "Oh, if only Sister Briege could come, if Sister Briege could only lay her hand on this person, it would happen." People can make you feel guilty that you can't be everywhere and that you can't pray with everyone.

In this Gospel story, the centurion believed that all he had to do was ask Jesus, that Jesus wasn't limited.

Indeed, Jesus is not confined to one place. God is everywhere and if I believe that Jesus is God, then I have to believe that his power is limitless and there is no distance with him.

This has helped me greatly in the ministry of healing. I don't have to run around and go to all the places where sick people are. Through my telephone ministry, I'm praying with people from one end of the world to the other by phone. I'm not with them, but I can unite with them and do exactly what the centurion did with Jesus. We can come together spiritually before God and healings can happen.

Some years ago, I was in Mexico. I went to the hospital to pray with a priest who had cancer. The priest was very, very ill. I said a brief prayer and I left the hospital.

The following day, as I was ministering to a large group of priests, a lady came in and interrupted us. She said, "I just got a phone call from the hospital saying that Father is dying."

As the woman told us the news, I spontaneously asked the priests to join together in prayer. I didn't think what I did was extraordinary. It was very natural to me that we should pray.

The very next morning, the gospel for the day was the story of the centurion's servant's healing. The priest who read the gospel told us what went through his mind when the news came about the dying priest. He said, "When the lady came in and said that Father was dying, I thought that Sister Briege would have to go to him."

The priest said at that moment an inner voice said to him, "I don't need Sister Briege at the hospital, but what I need from you and from Sister Briege is that you believe in my power."

He said that he became aware he must not limit Jesus to Sister Briege, that Sister Briege was just an instrument. What God had me doing at that moment—teaching and sharing with these priests—was what God wanted me to be doing. Just because I am limited physically to one place, I should never limit the Lord.

A year later, I got a phone call from a priest who said to me, "Sister Briege, I just read a beautiful testimony in a Mexican magazine about a priest you prayed with who was totally healed and is back teaching in college."

He read the testimony to me, and as he read it, it's as if I heard the Lord say, "Remember. Because you believed and because you trusted, this priest was healed." And it was like reliving the centurion's servant's story.

Another time, at a healing service in Scotland, I told the people, as I always do, "It is not necessary for me to pray with individuals. All of us here believe that Jesus lives in us. We are all called to be channels of love. And it is the Lord's love for us that heals us."

I invited the people to intercede for their loved ones who were not present at the healing service. "Ask Jesus to reach out and touch them, just as the centurion begged Jesus to touch his servant boy."

One of the women present had a sister in Ireland who, the next day, was going into the hospital to have a cancerous growth removed. The woman, during this healing service in Scotland, prayed for her sister in Ireland. At the same time in

Ireland, the Lord started ministering to the woman with cancer. Three weeks later, in Ireland, I met the woman. She told me she didn't know that her sister in Scotland was praying for her, but when she went into the hospital, the growth was completely gone. She was healed.

This was yet another confirmation that the Lord can heal at a distance, that we should never limit the Lord.

There is another lesson from the same Scripture passage in Matthew 8: the power of intercession.

What was this centurion doing? He came before Jesus and he interceded on behalf of his servant boy. He begged Jesus to heal him. It is one of the great examples of the need for us to believe when we pray.

My Auntie Lizzie has been a great source of inspiration to me and a great source of joy in my life. As she tells the story, a lady came to her house in Ireland to see me. I wasn't home, so Auntie Lizzie decided she would evangelize this person herself.

The woman, as they do in asking for me in my home town, asked Auntie Lizzie, "Is the nun home?"

My aunt replied, "The nun isn't here, but you don't have to see her. Just write down your intentions and she will intercede for your intentions with Jesus."

The lady said, "Fine, give me the book."

She started writing. There were two busloads of people outside that the lady had brought with her from the other side of Ireland. She stood there for an hour and a half writing down their intentions as they shouted them through the bus windows.

"Paddy, where does it hurt you? Mary, what's wrong with you?"

Auntie Lizzie was getting a little tired just standing there, so she said to the lady, "You know, you should talk to God yourself. You should ask Jesus yourself, and intercede."

The lady looked at Auntie Lizzie and she said, "Intercede? Talk to God? I've been talking to God for forty years and he's never heard me yet!"

Auntie Lizzie said back to her, "Well, maybe you're not talking to him the right way."

The lady said, "Well, I only know one way. Do you know any other way?"

Later Auntie Lizzie told me, "Oh, you'd better do your evangelizing yourself because I ran out of answers after she asked me that!"

But isn't it true that many people say they've talked to God for forty years and he hasn't heard them yet? But they haven't listened to him.

Jesus does answer us, but it may not be right away. The prayer of intercession is not always answered immediately. Another story shows the importance of intercessory prayer and how we must persevere in prayer.

Some time ago, when I was giving a couples' retreat, a gentleman came to me. He was terribly distraught because his marriage was in great difficulty. He and his wife were becoming involved in many different things and couldn't relate to each other. To further complicate the situation, he had evidence that his wife had been unfaithful. He had gone to a marriage counselor who told him to give her an ultimatum and if that didn't work, to get a divorce.

The man said it shattered him because he just couldn't accept divorce as an answer to his problem. He didn't know what to do.

I brought him into the church before the tabernacle. The Lord gave me a word for him: that it would get worse, but it would get better. This wasn't a very consoling word for me to give this poor man.

I told him that this would be a test of his faith, that sometimes we have to persist in prayer and in interceding for someone. I explained that when we intercede for others, God can work in our lives, too, and we can come to believe that miracles do happen. I told him that an increase in faith was one benefit of persevering prayer.

After this, he would travel long distances or phone me to

have me pray with him. All I would ever do was say to him, "Let's pray and don't give up."

He'd say to me, "I love my wife." He felt in his heart that the Lord did not want him to walk out of his wife's life, that their marriage was blessed by the church, that it was a sacrament. But, at the same time, all of his counselors were saying, "I'd leave her."

Yet each time he spoke with me, I'd encourage him not to give up. I'd remind him that Jesus said nothing is impossible for the man who believes.

I sympathized with him, "It's a very difficult thing to identify with someone who keeps on rejecting you, but you identify with Jesus. Even to this day, Jesus loves us and we reject him all the time. He doesn't stop loving us. If you set out to heal your own marriage you couldn't do it. But you can ask Jesus to give you supernatural strength. This won't take away the suffering and the pain of rejection, but you will have the strength to persevere."

One day he phoned me and said, "Sister Briege, I want to thank you. God answered our prayer."

He then related to me a beautiful spiritual experience that he and his wife had. One evening, the two of them had sensed God's transforming presence as they were preparing for bed.

He had not had relations with his wife for some time because the knowledge of her unfaithfulness was a barrier to his expression of love. But when they were in bed that night, the Lord enveloped the two of them in his love and he recreated in them the love they had had when they were first married. He transformed them. Not only did he renew their marriage, but he gave them all of the gifts of the Holy Spirit.

The man said he wanted to come to see me. I happened to be in the city where he lived so I told him to come over. When he came to see me, he said, "Sister Briege, I hope this will not be an insult to you, but you were a great signpost to Jesus. Many days when I was going to my work, I felt like just going to a divorce court, thinking, 'Why should I live through this?' But every time I talked to you, you turned me around by pointing to Jesus. You didn't take me there, but you sure told me what Jesus could do. Today I thank you because that's what a signpost does—it doesn't take you where you want to go, but it points out the direction to go.

"I learned two lessons from all this," he said. "First, I can never take my marriage for granted. I loved my wife, but I never really told her. Second, I must never underestimate the power of prayer and the supernatural strength that comes through it."

Progressive Healing

Although many people think their prayers are not answered if they are not healed immediately and miraculously, I have learned that the Lord heals in many ways—and for his own reasons. He often heals over a long period of time. I call this "progressive healing." I have seen some moving examples of this kind of healing. The Gospels refer to this healing especially in two passages—Mark 8:22-26 and Luke 17:12-19.

In Mark 8 we have the story about the blind man who begged Jesus to touch him. Jesus took the blind man outside the village and he put spittle on his eyes and laid his hands on them. Then Jesus asked him, "Can you see?"

The man answered, "Well, I can see people but they look like walking trees."

Jesus touched him a second time and then he could see perfectly.

When I read this, I said to myself, "Well, Jesus is God. He didn't have to touch him twice. He could have healed him the first time." What struck me was that while healing may not be completed, from the moment we start praying, progressive healing starts within us. Maybe that man was walking around for a long time seeing people who looked like walking trees, and then he came back to Jesus for the second touch and total healing.

Why didn't the Lord heal him the first time? Jesus doesn't say why, but perhaps through progressive healing the blind man drew closer to God than he would have had he been healed immediately. The two-stage healing did make him seek out Jesus a second time. After he was completely healed, the Scriptures say, "He saw everything clearly." Could that mean that he saw Jesus clearly, through renewed spiritual eyes?

At a conference in the United States, a couple came to me with their little boy. Little David had a tumor on the brain and the doctor had given the child only seven months to live. The couple had five or six other children who were heartbroken over the thought of losing little David.

As I was praying with them, I realized that their whole hope was in Sister Briege: "If only Sister Briege would pray with us, then everything would be answered and David would be healed."

There are many stories in the gospels where people came to Jesus interceding for themselves or for their families or their children. I told them some of these stories from the gospels.

I said, "I can pray, but this little David is your child. God used you as a husband and wife to participate with him in bringing David into the world. Now you go home and you intercede with Jesus every night for his healing."

The father said to me, "Maybe Jesus doesn't want to heal him, or maybe it's not his will."

This common question leads many people to think that they shouldn't ask for a healing. There are two things I say about this. First, God's will always comes to pass, but with God's will comes a great sense of peace and a great strength to accept it. Some people say, "It's not God's will" as a cop-out, because they don't really believe God can do it.

Second, they're afraid of what it means if healing doesn't happen: "Have I failed?" Of course they haven't failed, but this notion comes from certain misconceptions about how faith effects healing.

I said to David's father and mother, "Just forget for a moment about God's will. If Jesus were standing here before you, what would you ask Jesus to do for David?"

The mother said, "Oh, I'd ask him to heal David because I love him."

"Well," I said, "you ask Jesus to heal him. Ask him every day. Don't you be making up Jesus' will for him. After all miracles do happen. Just tell him exactly how you feel and tell Jesus that you love little David and ask him to please heal him."

Many people say one thing to Jesus, but they think another thing. They think that they have to make Jesus feel good by saying nice things to him. You don't have to make Jesus feel good. He knows what you think anyway.

What Jesus wants is that each of us relate to him as a living person, as the Jesus who is compassionate and who loves us and who knows our suffering.

Jesus knows how we feel. He knows the love of a father and mother for their children. He knows that it wouldn't be normal for a mother and father to say, "God, take my child because he's yours." Jesus will give parents the strength to do that when the time comes, but they should never fail to intercede and to beg Jesus for the healing they so deeply desire for their children. Our teaching on prayer tells us to keep knocking at the door, keep persisting.

I told these parents to go home and to pray every night with David, to gather their other children, some of them teenagers, around them to pray.

The father said to me, "Sister, we're not too good at praying."

I said to them, "Just talk to Jesus. Even if it is only saying an Our Father and a Hail Mary slowly. Get the children to ask Jesus to heal little David and to tell Jesus they love him. As you pray, lay your hands on David."

I explained to them that the father, as head of the household, has real power to bless his children and should pray with them. His wife, as their mother, should pray for them as well.

About two years later, I met the father. I had not heard from them since the day we had prayed together for David.

He said to me, "Sister, I have a beautiful story to tell you." He went on to say that after they went home, they set a time each evening after supper to pray for little David. No one could leave the house until they gathered around David and had this time of prayer.

The parents got the children to ask Jesus to heal the child. They discovered their children didn't have a problem in asking Jesus to heal their little brother.

As the months went on, the child's tumor kept growing. The father kept getting discouraged. He'd say, "It's really not working." He was expecting something to happen instantly. But his wife persevered. She said, "No, let's keep going. Let's keep praying."

Suddenly, they realized that seven months had gone by and David was still alive. The growth was still growing, but David was not blind. They realized they had only been focusing on one thing—that the growth was getting bigger.

After about sixteen months, the growth started to get smaller. As they continued to pray with David, they watched the growth shrink until it completely disappeared and the doctor watched it with them.

The father said to me, "Now, Sister Briege, I'll tell you what happened because of David's healing. When David was healed, the doctor said, 'Whatever it is you've been doing, keep doing it because it's working. You did very well.'

"It was then I realized that during those two years our children were transformed. If instant healing had taken place, the other children would never have experienced the transformation."

He said that even after David was healed, the teenage children would never leave the house after supper until the family had prayed together. It had become a part of their life and they had become comfortable praying together as a family.

This is a great example of progressive healing. We may not get what we pray for right away, but the Lord heals us in his time, because there are many areas in our lives that he wants to put in order.

As we pray, God doesn't change. Prayer changes us, just as prayer changed that whole family from one that was not closely knit into a family who love the Lord and love each other.

In Luke 17:12-19, you will find the story about the ten lepers whom Jesus healed. The passage says clearly, "on their way they were healed." We don't have any idea how long they were "on their way," but it could have been weeks or even months. In any event, their healing did not occur "on the spot," so to speak. They left Jesus and later discovered they were healed. Only one could overcome the time and distance between Jesus' ministry and their healing; only one remembered to come back to thank Jesus. The others forgot.

Isn't it true that sometimes we pray for something and when it happens we just accept it and don't even say thanks? We forget that the Lord did answer our prayers because he did not answer them instantly.

We live in an age of instant tea and instant coffee and instant photos: it seems everything is instant. And we treat God the same. We think that if God doesn't give us what we want right away, then he isn't giving it to us at all.

There are those who say that if you pray for a healing, then you should announce a healing instantly. Let's say I pray for someone with a pain in the head. Some people believe that, for the pain to go away, they have to say it is already gone. This is just a glorified way of telling lies. If you still have the pain in your head, you are not healed.

There are times, such as in my own case, that the Lord does heal instantly. The Lord has his own reasons for healing one person instantly and another over a period of time.

I explain it this way. I believe that there are two kinds of healings. To me a *miracle* is something that happens instantly, and a *healing* is something that may be progressive, and may happen through medicine, through an operation, through continued prayer.

Once when I was giving a retreat with Fr. Kevin Scallon in Australia, I met a sister who had been crippled by polio. She had braces on her legs and a back brace. After Father Kevin administered the sacrament of anointing, she sat for eight hours in the chapel. During that entire period, she stayed in one position and her entire body was shaking. I felt sure that she was experiencing the beginning of a progressive healing. I went over to her and said, "Sister, God is healing you."

I read later in a magazine that daily for four months, as she rested, her whole body would begin shaking again. The doctor explained that her tissues and muscles that were withered because of the polio were being brought back to life. He told her she was in the process of being healed. The braces were removed.

The healing didn't happen the day she was anointed. It began that day and it continued. The last time I heard, it was still continuing. Her body, the doctor explained, was being reconstructed under the anointing of God.

Some people find it difficult to believe in miracles or healings. They always say, "It would be so easy to believe, if only I could see a miracle."

While in Japan giving a retreat, an Irish priest said to me, "Briege, it would be awful easy to believe if I could see a miracle."

I told him, "Father, the Lord uses you every morning to perform a miracle."

He said, "I know about the mass, but you know what I mean, if only I could see somebody healed if they were blind or had bad legs, it would be very easy to believe."

I said, "Oh, do you think it would, Father? I've seen a lot of people healed, but that doesn't make it any easier. I still have to keep praying and many times I find myself thinking, 'Oh, that person's so sick' and wondering if healing is possible."

He said to me, "Oh, I think I'd be different. I think if I could see a miracle, I would really believe."

About three days later, Fr. Frank Sullivan was meeting twelve of his Jesuit priests in the room I had been using for ministering to the priests. I came there and as I walked in they said, "Oh, Briege, come in and pray with us."

I prayed with all of them. Among these Jesuits there was an elderly French priest who had a very severe gangrene in his leg. The doctor had told him he should have the leg amputated. He asked the doctor to let him make the retreat and then he would go for the amputation.

Father Frank asked us to gather around and pray for healing.

The next morning, we were getting ready to go to breakfast. The French priest came up to me gesticulating and making all kinds of signs to me, pointing to heaven and to his heart and just carrying on. I couldn't speak French or Japanese; I just kept looking at him. I thought with a little inward smile, "This poor man's getting a heart attack or going mad." So, I just walked away.

I went in to breakfast and this same priest came running into the room with the legs of his trousers rolled up. He was showing everyone that his leg was perfectly healed.

Three seats down from me was my Irish friend. I looked over at him and said, "Father, there's your miracle you were talking about the other day."

The Irish priest looked at him, and then he looked at me, and he said, "My God, it's awful hard to believe! Did he have gangrene at all?"

Then I said to him, "See, Father, it doesn't make it easier to believe."

The moral of this story, I suppose, is that people who have faith don't need to see.

FOUR

The Healing Power of the Eucharist

I N LUKE 8:40-48, WE FIND A LITTLE WOMAN in a crowd looking at Jesus with great hope. For years, she had been desperate for a healing. No one had been able to heal her. She had heard of Jesus. She believed. She said to herself, "If I could just touch Jesus, I know I'll be healed."

The little woman went up in the midst of this crowd and she reached out and touched him. Many people were pressing against Jesus, according to the Scripture, all wanting to see him, to touch him. But this little woman had one thing in mind. She believed that if she touched him, she would be healed.

She touched him, and in one of the gospel accounts, Jesus turned around quickly and said, "Who touched me?"

The apostles asked, "What do you mean, who touched you? Everybody's pressing up against you!" But Jesus knew that someone was there who was not merely touching him physi-cally. Someone was there with a sense of expectancy, with the requirement we all should have when we come to Jesus— expectant faith.

Then Jesus looked at the woman as she came forward, and he said to her, "Because of your faith, you are healed."

Many people, when they read this Scripture passage, say

something like, "If I could just touch Jesus! Wouldn't it be
wonderful to come in contact with Jesus?" Or they say, "To live
when Jesus lived! To be able to go up to him! I'd really touch
him in faith, as that little woman did!"

We Catholics often forget we can do much more than merely
touch Jesus. As Catholics we believe we actually receive Jesus.
We put out our hand and we receive the body and blood of
Jesus.

The Lord comes, through the power of the ordained priest,
and takes possession of the bread and wine. Then, at the Lord's
invitation to "take and eat," we receive the Eucharist and the
Lord takes possession of us.

We often use the word "possession" for the devil, but as
Christians we have to see ourselves as children whom the Lord
possesses with great love.

As I look back to my earlier life in Ireland, I probably should
have had a greater appreciation for the Eucharist. The Irish
people, over the centuries, have paid dearly for their Catholic
faith. In Ireland, there are many reminders of how our
forefathers suffered to preserve the Eucharist and to pass it on
to us. Ireland is dotted with "mass rocks." During the times of
severe persecution, priests were not allowed to say mass. There
was a price on a priest's head.

They had to go off into the mountains, in secret, sometimes
during the dead of night, to offer mass. They would select a flat
rock, suitable to serve as an altar, and there celebrate mass.
That's why these rocks are called "mass rocks" and that's how
the people were able to have the mass during that terrible
persecution.

To this very day, those mass rocks are preserved. Every year,
there is a celebration at the mass rocks and the mass is offered
there.

There are many stories in our ethnic and national traditions
of people who suffered in days gone by to protect and preserve
the Eucharist.

Baptism in the Holy Spirit

Even with all that, it was only after my own physical healing that I got a new understanding of the Eucharist. After being "baptized in the Spirit," I experienced a spiritual awakening that helped me see more clearly the great gift the Lord has given us in the Eucharist and the other sacraments.

Many people may not be familiar with the term, "baptized in the Spirit." It is a term taken from Scripture, particularly Acts 2 and 11.

We receive the gift of the Spirit at baptism. We receive the Holy Spirit throughout our lives—at communion time and through all the sacraments.

It's like receiving a birthday gift. If I received a birthday gift and I got totally distracted by the pretty wrappings and never opened the gift, I could never use the contents. The contents are valuable, not the wrappings, the externals.

So it is with this release of the Holy Spirit. The Holy Spirit is given to us by Jesus himself. Jesus said, "I will send my Spirit and he will teach you all things and help you to understand." Baptism in the Spirit is opening up to the gifts we receive through baptism and becoming open to the power of the Spirit to understand the sacraments and the power of the sacraments. Baptism in the Spirit enables us to understand all the gifts given to us to enable us to grow in holiness. Through this baptism in the Spirit, the sacraments themselves take on greater meaning.

The sacraments are not given to us simply to talk about or brag about. The sacraments must be effective in our lives. We have to live the power of the sacrament. For example, if I receive Jesus in the Eucharist, I must reflect the Lord I have received in my daily life.

If I meet Jesus in the sacrament of reconciliation, I must reflect a repentant and forgiving life.

If I receive the Holy Spirit in the sacrament of confirmation to give me power to be a strong Christian, I certainly must call upon the Holy Spirit in times of spiritual confrontation.

If a couple receives the Holy Spirit through the sacrament of matrimony, they have received a sacrament that, like a river, is ongoing. Married people can stop, at any time of need, to draw strength from the Spirit in their sacrament, just as a thirsty person stops at a running stream to quench his thirst. Married Christians must recognize their sacrament as an ongoing source of strength to help them remain faithful to their vows and their mission in the world.

The sacrament of holy orders enables a priest to show the presence of Christ through his ministry and to bring Christ to people through the sacraments. Also, through the power of the Holy Spirit, this sacrament enables the priest to live fully the priestly vocation every day of his life. Holy orders is a sacrament that helps the priest or the deacon to renew, every day, his ordination commitment.

The sacrament of the anointing of the sick is much more than a ritual in which you go to the priest and he anoints you with oil. Through the Spirit, it is an encounter with Jesus the Healer. The power of this sacrament heals both spiritually and physically. Through it, Jesus also forgives all sin.

Baptism in the Spirit—not itself a sacrament, but more like an actual grace—enables us to understand and to experience all the gifts of the Spirit. All these gifts, including the ones St. Paul talks about in 1 Corinthians 12, are all operative in our lives when they are needed.

In my own baptism in the Spirit, on the day of my healing, the Eucharist took on a new meaning to me. Before that day, I put more emphasis on how I would receive Jesus and what I was going to do.

It wasn't until some years later that I realized the important aspect of the Eucharist is not what I do, but what Jesus does and what I allow him to do in me. I must let the loving Jesus heal me and transform me through his body and blood. It is not my effort alone, but his action, that transforms me.

What Jesus Can Do in the Mass

I realized this truth while attending an outdoor mass in a mountainous Latin American country. Many very poor people came to this mass. The priest was using an old table for an altar.

A little boy was brought there who was suffering from very severe burns and sores on his body. I remember thinking, "My goodness, there's really nothing that can be done. It's so bad. We have no doctors or medicine here."

I admired the priest. His faith in Jesus taught me that I must let Jesus do what only Jesus can do in and through the Eucharist—change our lives.

We prayed with the little boy, then the priest said to the old woman who had carried him to the mass, "Just leave him under the table here and let's continue with the celebration of the Eucharist."

As the mass progressed, I was overwhelmed at the participation of the people in the mass. I was impressed that the priest was so aware of what he was doing through this liturgy, that he was making the mass come alive for these poor people.

It was evident in this priest's manner that he was excited about the mass, that he had a deep and personal faith in Jesus. He actually transmitted this to the people who attended that outdoor mass.

As we approached the consecration, I had my eyes closed. When I opened them, I discovered that people were prostrate on the ground. They lifted up their eyes to adore the Lord. The look on their faces made me think, "They really believe that this is Jesus." Then when I looked at the sacred Host, in my own imagination, I got the most beautiful image of Jesus with his two hands out. He was smiling with great love and compassion. He was embracing these poor people and saying, "Come to me, all who are weary, and I will give you life and faith."

This was the moment that I realized in the depths of my heart, "Dear Jesus, this is really you. It may look like bread and a cup, but only you could think of such a creative way to make yourself present to your people."

After the mass, I went around to see how the little boy was. He had been placed under the table which served as the altar. But he wasn't there. I said to the woman who had brought him to the mass, "Where is he?"

She said, pointing to a group of children playing nearby, "There he is."

I looked at the child and he was fine. There wasn't a thing wrong with his little body.

I said aloud, but more to myself, "What happened to him?"

The old woman looked at me and said, "What do you mean, 'What happened?' Didn't Jesus come?"

During this mass as in all masses, the priest had put his hands over the bread and wine, and he called upon the action of the Spirit to make this action holy "that it may become the body and blood" of Jesus. When the priest said this prayer, the Holy Spirit came, but he of course was not limited to do only what the priest asked. The Spirit also put his power over the little boy and the boy was changed. He was healed and made whole.

That same day, at the beginning of mass, I also saw a little boy who had a terrible facial deformity. At the end of mass, his mother came running up to me with her child in her arms. She said, "Sister, look at my little boy." The boy's face was healed.

I was the one who was very surprised, but this priest had a great capacity to introduce the people to a living Jesus. Like the woman in the gospel, they came to Jesus with an expectant faith. They did not come simply to look at what the priest was doing or to be critical about how the priest preached or celebrated mass. This was their Eucharist. They were coming to participate with Jesus in a celebration that was being offered to his Father. They were becoming a part of this offering. For them, it was a living experience with Jesus.

I left that mountain with a completely new understanding of the Eucharist. It isn't only what I can do to bring people to mass so they can be very reverent and tell Jesus they love him. That's very good, but it's what Jesus can and wants to do for all of us, for the entire world. It isn't that Jesus needs us to come to mass, but we need Jesus.

That night I couldn't sleep. I was very disturbed. I felt as though God were trying to tell me something. About four o'clock in the morning, I was still awake. I was turning and twisting. So, I got up and knelt at the side of the bed and said, "Jesus, what is it that you want to say to me?"

I felt the Lord saying to me, "You must make me known in the Eucharist. People are coming to you. People will come from all over looking for healing. They will say, 'Oh, if only we could get Sister Briege to touch us' or 'If Sister Briege could only lay hands on us, then we'd be healed.'

"Many are making false gods out of people in healing ministries. They are seeking after people and not me. I come every day in the Eucharist. I promised to give you life and to give it to you more abundantly, to fill you with strength for your pilgrimage.

"I want you to go out now into the world and point to me in the Eucharist. I want you to tell people to take their eyes off Briege McKenna and fix their gaze on their eucharistic Lord, to put their faith in me. You can disappoint them, and you will disappoint them, as will any person who attracts people to themselves. But if you point them to me, then they will never be disappointed."

Again, this showed me that I had to be a signpost, pointing to Jesus. From this experience in prayer, I began centering my teaching on the Eucharist.

Faith, Not Feelings

People began coming up to me saying, "I don't feel a thing at mass. It's boring. I get much more out of going to a prayer meeting where it's full of life and I feel so good."

I always respond, "Faith and feelings are two different things. There is no place in the word of God where Jesus said, 'By your feelings, you will be saved' or 'By your feelings, you will be healed.' He did commend people on their faith. Faith is believing in what we don't see. Jesus said, 'Blessed are those who do not see and yet believe.'"

This is the great challenge to us as Catholics. We can't explain the Eucharist because it is a miracle and a mystery. What counts is not understanding in the head, but believing in the heart. Feelings do not make Christ present in the Eucharist. It's the power of the Holy Spirit working through the ordained priest that makes Christ present to us in the Eucharist. I may feel nothing, but Jesus is still there.

On the other hand, I could go to a prayer service and take a piece of bread and try everything to make Jesus present, but that will not make him present. It requires the power of ordination.

Sometimes I ask myself if I really believe that Jesus is present in the Eucharist. Do I believe that this is the gift that Jesus spoke about in John 6? Remember that many of Jesus' disciples and followers couldn't believe him when he said that to be saved they must eat his body and drink his blood.

It was easy to accept Jesus when he was performing miracles and when he was doing all kinds of signs and wonders, but it's hard to believe when you can't understand and when you can't see things with your own eyes. But that is the challenge for the Christian. We are called to believe that Jesus is there in the Eucharist and that he loves us.

The very same challenge that is given to us was given to the first disciples. It was even harder for them. They did not have our advantage: the knowledge that Jesus rose from the dead, the witness of the apostles after Pentecost, two thousand years of tradition.

Just imagine this scene. Here is Jesus, standing in his one-piece white robe. He is talking to all his disciples shortly after he has multiplied the loaves and fishes to feed their hungry bodies.

He tells them that he loves them. He is the Bread of Life. He is going to give himself to them as food. They must eat his body and drink his blood. He tells them they are only following after him because he fed them through a miracle, that he is truly the Bread that comes down from heaven. It was not the manna of Moses that saves them. This manna would not give them eternal life, but the Bread he would give comes down from the Father and gives eternal life. He tells them that he is that Bread. He tells them again and again that they must eat his flesh and drink his blood.

Read it. It's all in the Gospel of John, chapter 6.

Then comes the moment when the disciples begin to look at him. They find it difficult to believe what he is saying. How can they eat his flesh or drink his blood? What kind of teaching is this? This sounds pretty horrible. You are looking at this man and he tells you he is going to give himself to you as food.

Remember, this was before the resurrection. They were living with Jesus when he was in his physical body. He looked just like any other man because he was truly a man, truly human. He was asking them to believe a very difficult thing.

Many said, "Well, he was very sensible up until now, but do you hear what he's saying now to us? We're going to have to eat his flesh, that this is how we're going to get life!" Many just shook their heads and walked away from Jesus.

What did Jesus do? Did he follow them and say, "Aw, don't go away. You misunderstand me. I'll explain it later"? Did he say, "I'll make it easier for you to believe. I don't really mean what you think I mean"?

He didn't say that at all. Do you know what he did? He let them go. He was saddened that so many questioned him and would no longer walk with him.

Then he turned to those men who would be empowered to make him available to his church as food. He challenged them: "What about you? Would you, too, like to leave?"

He didn't make it easy for them. Can you imagine the poor disciples? They truly loved him. But they must have been thinking, "This is surely hard to accept." Peter, the one Jesus would choose to lead his people, spoke on behalf of the rest of the disciples. In chapter 6 we read that he looked at the Master and he said, even though he couldn't possibly understand what Jesus meant, "Whom can we go to? We are convinced and we have come to believe that you are the Son of God!"

They accepted it. They accepted Jesus and loved him so much so they could believe what he said, even if they could not understand how it would happen.

In harmony with the faith of the Catholic church and the teachings of the magisterium, every Catholic must be able to say the words of Peter: "To whom can we go? We are convinced and we have come to believe that you are the Son of God."

I believe, as a Roman Catholic, that the Vicar of Christ authentically represents the mind of Christ. There may be many things he teaches that we do not understand or find difficult to accept. There are some things that we, as Catholics, may say we cannot accept because they are too hard.

I thank God for giving me the faith to be able to look at Pope John Paul and say, "Yes, I believe he is the one chosen by Jesus Christ. I love the Catholic church and I believe." I am convinced that the Lord will honor our faith, as he did that of the apostles. He will honor our obedience to his word spoken through the magisterium of the church, our faithfulness to the traditions, teachings, and dogmas of our faith.

We need to think about what Jesus did after Peter professed faith in him. He didn't just talk and do nothing. His was a prophetic teaching. If you read John 6, you will see that Jesus did not say, "Well, this looks like holy bread," or "This bread will be blessed." No, he said, "This is the living bread come down from heaven. He who eats my flesh and drinks my blood will have everlasting life." And in the Passover accounts in Matthew, Mark, and Luke, Jesus says, "This is my body which will be given for you. This is the blood of the new covenant which will be shed for many for the remission of sin."

The mass and faith in the Eucharist have nothing to do with feelings. I'm sure the apostles didn't feel anything great when they were challenged to that faith, to believe something they had not yet seen or could not possibly understand. So it is with us as we go to mass. We come to the Eucharist every Sunday with the faith of Peter and say, "I believe that this is the living Christ who has come down upon our altar today. I am actually going to receive him."

Another insight helps me embrace the great mystery of the Eucharist. Take the example of a television. I can watch an event, like the Olympics, even months after it has happened, and get as excited as if I were there at the time it actually occurred. I can strain with the runners and swimmers and cheer with the crowds. I can find myself on the edge of my chair rooting for my favorite athlete. As I watch such an event, it is as though I am really living it.

I believe that through the mass, through the power of the Holy Spirit, we are actually reliving, in an unbloody way, the sacrifice of Calvary, the passion, death, and resurrection of Christ.

Jesus suffered only one time. He went through his passion, death, and resurrection only one time. As it says in Hebrews, the Jewish priests were continually offering sacrifice to cleanse them of sin and to make reparation. But Jesus offered one sacrifice, and it was sufficient to cleanse and bring redemption to the world, to all peoples of all time. That one sacrifice we live daily with Jesus through this tremendous miracle of the mass.

If I truly believe I meet Jesus fully alive in the mass, I realize that I meet him in two very concrete and powerful ways. I meet Jesus through the proclamation of the word of God. The deacon or the priest who proclaims the gospel to me is actually serving me a living word that will cleanse me, heal me, and free me. When I receive the Eucharist, I receive food for my soul.

At the table of the Lord, I receive direction and guidance for my pathway through life. In the Eucharist, I receive food to strengthen me to live out what I just heard proclaimed in the gospel.

Touching Jesus in the Eucharist

Thinking of meeting Jesus in these two ways and reminded again of the story of the woman who touched the hem of Jesus' garment, I want to share a couple of incidents that illustrate this gospel theme.

One is the story of a young priest. He phoned me, very anxious and afraid. He had just found out he had cancer of the vocal chords and he had to have his voice box removed in three weeks. He was telling me he was desperate. He had been ordained only about six years.

As I prayed with him, I felt the Lord wanted me to tell him about the Eucharist. I said, "Father, I can pray with you now on the phone, and I will, but this morning, didn't you meet Jesus? Don't you meet him every day?"

What I didn't know was that this priest didn't celebrate mass daily.

I told him, "Father, every single day when you go to mass, when you take that sacred Host, when you eat it, you meet Jesus. The woman only touched the hem of Jesus' cloak. But you touch Jesus and receive him into your body. You have him as food. Do you realize that Jesus is actually going down through your throat? There is no better one to go to than Jesus. You ask Jesus to heal you."

I heard him crying over the phone. He kept saying to me, "Oh, Sister, thank you. Thank you."

Three weeks later, he went in for his surgery. He phoned me later to tell me that he didn't have the surgery. The doctors discovered the cancer was gone and he had brand new vocal chords.

I never even found out his name. About a year later, I got word about him, through a friend of his. Before his illness, this young priest had stopped celebrating mass except on Sunday; he had been very flippant about the mass. God used this experience of cancer to transform his life. This priest was totally healed, but not only physically. He became a Eucharist-centered priest. The Eucharist became for him a time to meet the living Jesus, like the woman at the well in John 4. He started to meet Jesus at the greatest of all wells, where you drink and you never thirst. Yes, miracles do happen.

Another healing involving the Eucharist happened in

Sydney, Australia. A woman came to a place where Father Kevin and I were speaking. She came up to me in a hallway to ask me to pray with her. She was desperate because she was suffering from stomach cancer. She had a tumor which caused great swelling. The doctors had told her there was little point in operating because it had spread too extensively.

I knew there was a mass that afternoon, so I told her I'd pray with her, but I also told her to go to mass and to ask Jesus to heal her.

Her main concern was fear of death. She said, "Sister, I'm so scared of dying. If only God would take away this awful fear that I have!"

I told her, "Go to meet Jesus in the Eucharist. While I can't tell anyone they will be healed the way they want because I'm not God, Jesus will supply you the strength to face whatever is on your road of life. If he is going to bring you through the door of death, he will give you the grace to go through that door without this awful fear. And if you are to live, he will give you the grace to live."

Unknown to me, she had also gone to Father Kevin and he had told her the same thing.

That was early in the day, on a Saturday. That night, when we were having a rally, a woman came running up the aisle of the hall and she threw her arms around me saying, "Sister, it happened! It happened!"

I wondered who this woman might be and what had happened.

I asked her, "What happened?"

She said, "Look at me. I came to you this morning. I went to mass as you said. When I was walking up to communion, I said to myself, 'In a few minutes, I am going to meet Jesus. I'm going to take him in my hand and I will ask him for his help.'"

While she was a Catholic who received communion often, this time she looked at the sacred Host and said, "I know you are really here. Today when you come into me, take away this fear. Heal me if you want, but please do something for me."

She told me, "I had no sooner put the Host on my tongue

and swallowed it than I felt as though something was burning my throat and down into my stomach. I looked down at my stomach and the growth was gone."

That woman was healed. I wonder how many of us come to the Eucharist only physically present, without any expectant faith, any excitement over what we are doing. Perhaps we come to the Eucharist only for what we get out of it and we do not thank God or praise him for giving himself to us.

Faith is a decision. We have to put effort into it. One might say about the mass, "I don't understand it, I don't feel a thing, but I believe it."

If you come to mass with the right attitude, your life will change. Our churches are often packed with people who come and leave the same way. You ask yourself, "Is it Jesus? Did he change? Is he not fulfilling his promises?" Or could it be that I do not have the expectant faith to allow him to touch my life and answer my needs?

He's the same Jesus yesterday, today, and forever. He is the Jesus who healed in the gospel. So he must be fulfilling his promises of answering his people's needs.

We can blame the priest for our lack of faith when we say the priest is boring or not charismatic or too loud or too timid, but the priest is not really the issue. The real issue is our own faith. It's true that if the priest has great faith, it is a great step toward meaningful worship. That's why, in my ministry to priests, I always challenge the priests to greater faith.

We have to look beyond ourselves and beyond the priest's humanity to see what he represents at the mass and what he is doing. As a Catholic, I know I must not let the priest come between myself and Jesus in the Eucharist.

The church obliges us to attend mass, not because Jesus needs us, but, like all good mothers, the church knows we need the Bread of Life to live in a world that Jesus himself told us would hate us, because it hates him.

We need to be strengthened for our journey. Food for soul and food for body: this is what he gives us in the mass.

FIVE

Chosen from among Men

GOD IS A GOD OF GREAT LOVE. He provides for us in every way. He has given to us the sacraments to enable us and to strengthen us in our pilgrimage through this life.

While it is not possible here to speak of every sacrament in detail, I would like to reflect with you on one sacrament, one that affects all our lives, one that is under severe attack at this point in history. I am speaking of the sacrament of holy orders, the sacrament of the priesthood.

Because the priesthood is under such severe attack, it needs, perhaps more than ever before, our encouragement and support which is rooted in our gratitude to God for his great goodness.

For all of us, priests and laity—people on a journey—this sacrament is another beautiful expression of God's faithfulness to provide and fulfill his prophetic teachings for us in our times.

The priesthood is a gift through which every Catholic is affected. It is through this sacrament of holy orders that we are enabled to receive the Bread of Life. It is through this sacrament that we receive the sacrament of the sick and the sacrament of reconciliation.

Besides these specific sacraments, these undeniable moments of communion with the life-giving, forgiving, and healing

Jesus, the priesthood touches us in so many beautiful ways. For example, the priest is there when we grieve. He is there for weddings, when we are filled with joy and hope. He is there as a father, to advise, to direct, to encourage.

The priesthood affects every one of our lives. The priesthood affects even the lives of people who do not go to church, for the parish priest prays daily for all the people of the church, for the conversion of sinners, for the reconciliation of people alienated from the church. He leads the entire community of faith in praying for peace, for the poor, for sinners.

It is because of this, and the fact that our priests are under attack, that I want to share and reflect on the sacrament of holy orders.

As a young sister, I had the great privilege to come under the influence of a very holy woman, Mother Agnes O'Brien, O.S.C. She was the mother general of our congregation.

Mother Agnes had a great reverence and love for the priesthood. She often spoke with great gratitude to me about the priesthood. During the hours I spent with her during her illness, God was preparing me for the mission he would give me years later, especially for my work with priests.

Attacks on the Priesthood

In the early 1960s, many changes took place in the church because of the Second Vatican Council. These changes had a dramatic effect on the priesthood. Attitudes toward the priesthood also changed. Until recently, the priest was put on a pedestal and we kept him up there because it was safe to have him there. We didn't want him to come off that pedestal because it would be too challenging to us.

The priest was removed from the people in many ways. He was often the only learned man in the community. He was the one that people automatically sought out for any need. People believed that he was a man of God, a man who was chosen.

In recent times, we have more freely criticized priests. There was a lot of turmoil and many priests left the priesthood. I found myself, in the early 1970s, at the beginning of the healing ministry, becoming very judgmental and critical of certain attitudes and opinions among the clergy.

One day in the chapel, with all this on my mind, I asked the Lord, "What is wrong with the priesthood?"

The answer came back to me, "What do you mean, what's wrong with the priesthood? Have I ever given a gift that is not perfect? What have you done and how have you thanked me for this gift of priesthood that affects your life and all mankind?"

It was then that the Lord revealed to me that I couldn't just sit back and criticize the priesthood. Actually, in the sacrament of holy orders, the priest says yes to God so he can be a priest for me, for you, for every one of us.

Jesus led me into what seemed to be a sequence of images appearing over the tabernacle. There I saw the ordination of a priest—through the Lord's eyes.

When we look at a tapestry hanging on a wall, we see only the finished results of the labor of the artist. We do not see all the labor and love that went into its making. However, on the reverse side, we see all the different threads and stitches and labor that went into the making of the beautiful work of art.

So, too, when we look at a priest, we see the obvious strengths and weaknesses. But we do not see behind the scenes where the Lord has, with love and faithfulness, endowed the soul with a priestly vocation and guided him to ordination.

I found myself weeping as I watched the unfolding of this powerful revelation of the priesthood and what it means to a man to be ordained to the priesthood. I had a sense that everyone in heaven—Mary, the angels and all of the saints—were praising God's faithfulness to humanity in his call to men in every age to give them the power to make him present among his people.

Through this experience, I got a new understanding of the priesthood. I got a new love and a deep reverence for the sacrament of holy orders. I came to understand that the priesthood is not something that I can acquire through human means, not a gift that I can demand to make me equal to others. It has nothing to do with equality. It's like any gift. Gifts are not something that I can force or demand. A gift is freely given. God gives this gift out of his generosity. He gives this power— his power—to humanity, to enable us to feed on him, the Bread of Life.

It was with this great sense of gratitude for the priesthood that the Lord then led me to the understanding of what he was asking of me that morning.

He showed me a group of very hungry people. The Lord said, "Do you see these people? They come to you because they are looking for help, for healing. They come to you because they are hungry. A time is coming when there will be a great famine and they will hunger for the Bread of Life. I am that Bread of Life."

He then allowed me just a glimpse into what was coming. People would turn against the priesthood and begin to see it only as a job. He showed me a priestly vocation as a little seed he sowed in the hearts of many young men, but the seed was not nurtured so it could not grow and bear fruit.

God revealed to me that a time was coming when families would no longer see the priesthood as a gift they would want for their sons. We would create an environment that was removed from God, pagan and materialistic, rooted in the wisdom of the world. Because of this society, young men, given the seed of a priestly vocation, would not be able to respond. The seed would lie dormant. They would not hear the call muffled by materialism and parental apathy.

Little by little, where the priesthood would not be appreciated, where it would be attacked and go undefended by Catholic people, it would die. It would die, not because the gift was not given, but because we refused it, because we didn't want it, because we had chosen the false gods of materialism and watered-down religion.

I became aware that there would be many attacks through

gossip and criticism. This gossip and criticism adds fuel to the fire. The difficulties some priests experience are bad enough, but many Catholics add to the scandal by broadcasting the bad news to family and friends, falling into the plan of the Evil One to destroy further the sacred gift of priesthood. This attitude adds to the difficulties of priests struggling against sin in their lives.

I felt the Lord telling me, "I want you to go into the world to tell my people that the priesthood is their gift, so they may be fed and strengthened. I want you to call them to intercede, to love my priests, to reverence this sacrament. When my people love, reverence, and are grateful for the priesthood, priestly vocations will flourish in their midst. It will be a joy for young men to say yes to this call because they will be supported by their communities and by their families."

My first mission was to go into the world to call the laity and the priests to recognize the importance and power of this sacrament. From apostolic times, we have been blessed by God with priests who make Jesus present to us in the Eucharist and in the proclamation of his Word.

Down through the ages, the forces of evil have tried to destroy the priesthood. We can read story after story of how priests in Communist countries have been destroyed, put in prison, and martyred.

And even in so-called Christian nations, we see the rise of anticlericalism. Today some people gloat over the news about a priest who leaves his vocation or causes some sort of public scandal. There seems to be a triumphant spirit as people cynically brag, "Well, there goes another priest."

Attacks against the priesthood are attacks against all of us as Catholics. It was with this realization that I heard the Lord say, "You must tell my people that the Evil One is deceiving all of you when you begin to reject this gift of priesthood, when you begin to try to put it on a human level, when you say that it is just a job, a profession."

The second mission was made clear in an image that touched

me very deeply. It was as if I was standing beside Jesus and he let me look out over the city of Jerusalem. The city was filled with bishops and priests. Suddenly Jesus began to weep. He said to me, "Briege, these are the men I have chosen to shepherd my people, to feed my people, to encourage my people, to lead my people. They are losing faith in me. They are seeking the wisdom of the world. They are denying my power and choosing earthly power." He revealed to me there would be a great crisis in the priesthood. Priests would lose faith in Jesus and fail to acknowledge his power working through them in holy orders.

I sensed God asking me to go into the world and remind bishops and priests with this word. "It is not humility to deny the power of the priesthood, but it is humility to acknowledge that I have chosen them. I have chosen them not because they are holy, not because they are better than others, but I've chosen them because of my mercy, love, and compassion for humanity. It is because of this mercy, love, and compassion, that I use them to make myself present. But how I long to do it more effectively through them! Go out and tell them to believe in me."

As I got up to leave the chapel, after nearly four hours, my attitude had changed. God, in the twentieth century, is still giving us the gift of priesthood.

My attitude changed toward the humanity of the priest. I became much more aware of the need to pray for priests, that they are truly men of faith.

Teaching Children about the Priesthood

I decided to start in my first-grade class. Every day I prayed with them and talked with them about the priesthood. I had a priest, Fr. Harold Cohen from New Orleans, come in to celebrate mass for the children and to explain to them what the Eucharist meant. I asked him to explain the difference between their dad and the priest, how the priest was called to be a father but in a different way than their fathers, that he had to give his whole life to Jesus so the Lord could minister through him. Father Harold had brought to the classroom a candle and a basket. He told them the Gospel story about not hiding your light under a bushel, that a priest was a man who brought light to the world.

Father Harold explained what would happen when he held his hands over the host and chalice and asked the Spirit to come so the Lord could be truly present.

After mass, I asked the children if anyone could tell me the definition of a priest. One little boy held up his hand and said, "A priest is a guy who lights other guys' candles."

Isn't it true that the priest does bring the light of Christ to all his brothers and sisters in the world?

It was these little first graders that made me realize the power of prayer and the need to pray for priests. It was through these first graders that I witnessed the first great healing in a priest.

I had met a priest at a prayer meeting. He was going through a very difficult crisis and was about to leave the priesthood. I promised I would get the first graders to pray for him.

I had the children pray. They decided to write the priest. Since I hadn't explained his problem, but had only asked the children to pray for his healing, they thought he was ill or had been in an accident. Their letters and drawings depicted the priest in bed with his leg in a cast and with bandages on his head.

A couple of months later, the priest called me and said he wanted to make a special trip to Florida just to talk to the children. He came and he brought their letters with him—and a big bag of candy which, of course, pleased the children very much.

He told them he had been going through a bad time, that he had stopped talking to Jesus and because of their prayers, he was going to keep on being a priest and now he was good friends again with Jesus.

Later he told me that, particularly, the letter of one five-year-old girl had touched him deeply. In the letter she said that I had told them he was sick. She said, "I know you can't do the things that Jesus wants you to do right now. But we've asked Jesus to help you. You are very special to Jesus. We know Jesus will make you better. We need you and love you. We hope when you're well you can come to see us."

As the priest read her letter, it pierced his heart and the Lord spoke to him, "This little child understands. This little child knows what your priesthood is. But do you really know?"

He told me that it was then that he started to pray and his life changed.

This was a great joy to me because it confirmed what Jesus had told me in the chapel—that if I would get people to pray and intercede, priests would be renewed.

A few months after receiving the image in the chapel, Fr. Cohen phoned me and asked me to help him give a priests' retreat.

My immediate reaction was, "Father, I couldn't go on a priests' retreat. I'm a first-grade teacher. There is no way I could go. It would not be possible. My principal couldn't let me off."

I made all these excuses because I was afraid. Fr. Cohen said, "You know, Briege, it wouldn't do the priests any harm to be first graders for a change. I think the Lord wants you to come."

I went to my principal and to my surprise she said, "Briege, I think it would be a great idea for you to go."

I was frightened. I had never before given a talk to priests. I found out that many of these men didn't want to be on this retreat. They had been asked to come by their bishop to learn more about the charismatic renewal. They weren't that interested in the renewal and the idea of a nun on this retreat didn't add to their enthusiasm.

As I listened to Fr. Cohen in his introductory talk say that the Holy Spirit would give the retreat, I thought, "I sure hope he is because I'm so scared."

The next morning, to my great horror, Father Cohen was quite ill. He told me I would have to carry on the retreat and he encouraged me by his confidence in me. In spite of my great fear and nervousness, the Lord did use me.

I found myself experiencing a deeper love, compassion, and gratitude for these men. For the first time ever, I heard the stories of priests in their humanity. I heard their cries for help, to be loved, to be affirmed. I saw their loneliness and their need for ministry.

It seemed that the Lord put into those forty priests every problem I was ever going to meet in my ministry to priests. It was like a crash course in the priesthood.

Now, many years later, I look back. I have traveled throughout the world ministering to priests. I have had the opportunity to speak to lay people and religious. The two missions have become a reality.

Happily, I find many people beginning to intercede and to pray for priests. The grace to love and encourage priests is a growing reality among more lay people and religious around the world.

The Challenge to Faith

Some people might think the greatest need in the priesthood is a change in the church's celibacy ruling. But if I were asked today what is the greatest need in the priesthood, I would say a deep living faith.

I'd like to challenge priests in their call: to greater faith, but also to greater hope and love.

As I challenge priests, I challenge laity as well, because from baptism we all share in the royal priesthood of Christ. St. Peter calls us a priestly people (1 Pt 2:5-9). We need each other, priests and laity. We need to encourage each other in our mission in the church—in the ministerial priesthood and in the baptismal priesthood of the faithful.

It is essential that the priest be a man who believes in Jesus Christ. When Jesus called his first disciples, he called them and invited them to come with him. In the three years that he spent with them, he transformed their minds from the standards of the world to his own. He called them to believe that there was nothing impossible with him.

He gave them opportunities to grow in faith by challenging them in impossible situations, such as feeding thousands with five loaves and two fish, walking on the water, and going out to heal the sick and drive out demons.

The same challenges are offered to priests of our world today. The priest must believe. He is not sent out to defend Jesus or make excuses for him. He is sent out to proclaim him. I've often told priests that when a man in the business world is selling a product he has to believe in it or people won't buy it. It's the same with the good news. If a priest doesn't believe in it, people will not be convinced.

One priest I know went down to Latin America, eager to help the poor. He had great enthusiasm. He had the material means to alleviate the poverty and hunger of the people there.

When he got to Latin America, he began to build clinics and schools. After ten years, he noticed that many of his parishioners were going to a mission established by some evangelicals.

One day he complained to one of the old men, a very faithful old man who was always around the church and helping the priest. The old man looked at him with tears in his eyes and said, "Father, I don't want to hurt you, but I have to tell you. You brought us a lot of good things. You have worked very hard, but you didn't bring us Jesus and we need Jesus."

The priest said, "I was ashamed. It was then I realized that I had decided to give them all they needed for their bodies, and then I would celebrate with them and preach for them. I was so busy, I didn't celebrate mass. I was a working priest. I didn't have time. It was important to feed these people. They were hungry. Yet the Lord showed me, through the very people for whom I had spent all my energies, that they wanted more than material things."

1. Little Briege McKenna, age 6. Taken at Jonesboro School, County Armagh.

2. The future Sister Briege made her first communion in 1952 with her brother, Peter.

3. Briege, age 11, with two brothers, a cousin and pet goat.

1. Sister Briege's parents, George and Brigid McKenna.

2. A proud father, George McKenna, posed with his daughter, Sister Briege, on the day of her final vows in 1967.

3. Sister Briege with Sister Mary Brendan, her novice mistress, and Sisters Mel and Seraphine.

1. In Medugorje, Yugoslavia, Sister Briege spoke with Vicka Ivankovic, one of the youth who have had visions of Mary.

2. Ivan Dragicevic, another Medugorje visionary.

3. Father Tomislav Vlasic of Medugorje, and Sister Briege. In Rome, she had a vision of him and the church in Medugorje.

4. A man holds up a boy whose gangrenous legs were miraculously healed during Mass in a Third World nation.

5. Sister Briege and Father Rick Thomas pray over the poor of El Paso/Jaurez.

In Brasilia, the capitol of Brazil, Sister Briege and Ingrid Orglmeister, her interpreter, pray with the military.

In July, 1985, Sister Briege led a retreat for priests in the Archdiocese of Porto Alegre, Brazil.

In 1982, Pope John Paul II greets Sister Briege McKenna at the Vatican following a private Mass in the papal chapel.

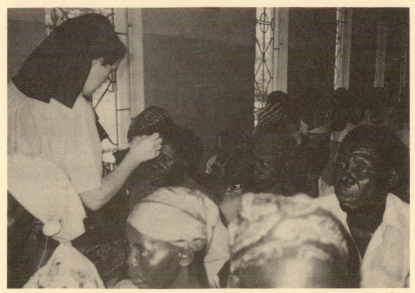

Sister Briege prays with lepers in Nigeria in February 1987.

It was then that the Lord brought this priest out of Latin America and back to his own country. He attended a prayer meeting and heard a little old lady give a teaching that would change his life.

She recalled that Jesus said, "Man does not live on bread alone but on every word that comes from the mouth of God" (Mt 4:4). When the priest heard this, he again realized it was his responsibility to build the kingdom of God. Material things are important, but the priest cannot become a social worker or a politician. He cannot depend on human resources. His resource must be Jesus Christ.

When his spiritual blindness was taken away, this priest said, "Sister, I had lost my faith. I had become angry when I saw the poor exploited; I couldn't see anything else." That priest went back to Latin America a changed man. He had encountered the living Jesus. He began to see that the first thing he must do is preach the gospel.

I work very much in Latin America and in many other parts of the world. I say to priests that to bring Jesus to our altars is the most beautiful thing they can do.

I ask them, "Do you really believe that you have the power, because of your ordination, to bring the living God down on earth? Do you have the faith that Mary had?"

When Mary said yes, she said yes to give birth, to give her whole body, her whole being to let Jesus come. It would be difficult because she had to die to her own plan; she had to die to what she could do and let God fulfill his will through her. She had to watch as God fulfilled his will through Jesus.

So it is with the priest. When he says yes to the priesthood, he has to die to that part of him that would want to do everything himself, that would want to straighten out the things that are wrong, that would want to change the oppressions and the oppressors. He has to die to himself and let Jesus, through him, be the answer to these problems. He must recognize that, like Mary, he gives birth to Jesus. Only he can bring Jesus to us through the Eucharist.

We need social workers and all the help people can give to the poor. We need all our lay missionaries and all our sisters, but we can never forget that we need, more than anything, the Bread of Life. We must have Jesus come among us. The poor and the oppressed must have the same opportunity to receive Jesus as do people in richer and freer nations. To deny them this is a terrible offense to God. This is the gift that God has given to them.

That is why faith is so important. It is important that when the priest experiences his helplessness and he wants to do things himself that he be able to say, "I must decrease so that he may increase" (Jn 3:30). He must realize that he can do nothing on his own but, as Paul said, "he who is within me can do infinitely more than I can imagine" (Eph 3:20).

That priest went back to Latin America as a changed man with his faith renewed. He began to understand the words that Jesus spoke to his apostles and was speaking to him today, "There is nothing impossible to me." He saw, through the eyes of faith, the importance of his call to the ministerial priesthood and he understood the need to rely on God, through prayer, for strength to fulfill his vocation.

This priest's experience recalls a quote from a lecture given by a Canon Patrick Augustine Sheehan to young Irish men near the turn of the 20th century. Canon Sheehan was a native of County Cork, a parish priest and prolific spiritual writer. He said: "As you see men seek their own ways and interest, beware at that moment for you will be tempted to forget or deny the sacred principles you have learned. You will be tempted to believe that your sacred office is not a mission and vocation, but a mere profession and that you are at liberty to introduce the language and customs and principles of the world into the sanctuary where maxims of the gospel alone should be recognized and accepted."

Daily, I thank Jesus for the priesthood. As I sit in my chapel before the Blessed Sacrament I thank him for the men who responded to his call.

One final thought about faith and priestly ministry. A priest, as I have said, gets his power from God in the sacrament of holy orders, from the Holy Spirit who speaks to him in prayer and to him through the church. His power comes from his union with God through prayer. He does not get power from theological studies or academic degrees. While study is important and while we need theologians and scholars, knowledge can never replace faith, can never replace being one with God through prayer and relying on him exclusively.

It is the power of Jesus Christ that converts and transforms people. The experience of the priest in Latin America, and of many others around the world, bears this out.

The Cure of Ars is a good example of a priest who relied solely on the power of his Lord. John Vianney was nearly refused ordination because he was such a poor student. Yet, once ordained and filled with the power of the priesthood, he became known by people throughout the world for his wisdom and pastoral insights in the confessional. People came to Ars, France, from throughout the world to confess to him, to ask him for prayer.

Priests should never feel inadequate because they may lack doctorates or other recognized educational achievements. Once ordained, the sacrament contains the power the priest needs for his mission in the church.

The Challenge to Hope

The second area of challenge for priests—and for all Christians—is hope. The priest is called to be a man of hope. Our Holy Father continually reminds priests and religious that they must be signs and symbols of hope in a world where hope is shattered daily.

People who have lost sight of God now build their hopes on governments, financial securities, and other people.

The only security and the only hope comes in Jesus.

I say to priests that it is good for us to look to Mary and the challenge this young Jewish woman had to face. Mary heard the beautiful words of Gabriel, that her child would be Son of the

Most High. She was deeply touched by the beautiful prophetic words, and yet she had to live through the soul-searing contradiction of Jesus' life. Her Son was born in a stable, lost when he was twelve, rejected by his people, treated like a criminal, beaten and spat upon, crucified and mocked. Through it all, she pondered the angel's words in her heart. She was willing to be steadfast in hope when hope seemed ridiculous.

Like Mary, the priest receives a promise when he is ordained. Like Mary, he must face many contradictions. Like Mary, he is called to hope when hope seems ridiculous.

As with faith, hope comes only through prayer. It is very important that we recognize faith, hope, and love as the branches that come forth from the vine.

A friend of mine, whose husband was dying, had a very disappointing encounter with a priest. Both Susan and her husband had great faith and believed Jesus would heal him.

The hospital chaplain, knowing the man was dying, came to visit him. He was surprised to find this dying man clinging to the hope that Jesus would heal him. The priest apparently did not believe that miracles do happen. He told the man he must prepare for death and said that a healing was out of the question.

The priest's words shattered all hope, and as a result, the man slid into a coma. The doctor sent for Susan.

Many hours later as Susan was sitting in the waiting room, the priest came in. She said to him, "Oh, Father, would you please pray for my husband. He's in a coma. Ask Jesus to heal him."

The priest told her, "I was in here earlier with your husband and I told him he was going to die and warned him about the dangers of false hope."

Susan realized it was the priest's lack of hope that caused her husband such distress.

She told the priest, "You don't need to worry about whether my husband and I can accept God's will. We know that we are going to die when God calls us. But Father, I don't think you are

called, as a priest, to tell people what Jesus can't do and take
away their hope. I just pray that what happened today will never
happen again because of your lack of hope."

The husband died a few days later. She never held that against
the priest. Susan understood that the priest was trying to
protect her and her husband from disappointment.

We all want to protect people from false hope. You can give
people false hope by pointing to yourself, but you can never
give them false hope by pointing to Jesus and telling them what
Jesus can do for them.

I tell priests they don't have to feel limited in the face of
hope-challenging situations. The gospel, in its very essence, has
power to bring hope. This is the power of the word of God.
Even when a priest is not preaching, through his faith-filled and
hope-filled words, he encourages people to turn to God. He is
imparting to them hope, the kind of hope Mary had in the
midst of her darkness.

The Challenge to Love

Finally, the priest must be a man of love. The greatest
commandment Jesus gave his disciples, that we must all follow,
is that we must love. The way to grow in holiness is to grow in
love of God and our neighbor.

This is the challenge for the contemporary priest. He is called
to reflect Christ in a radical way. We call him a "Christ-man."
He must reflect Christ in his love, gentleness, power, and
understanding. It is a very difficult call. It is impossible if the
priest tries on his own, but it's not impossible if he remains in
union with Christ, if he himself is a man of prayer. The priest is
called by God and God enables him to live a life of love.

It is important to see in what ways we, both laity and priests,
look at priesthood in the whole aspect of love in today's world.

I would like to look at the priest as a man of love in terms of
unity, celibacy, fatherhood, and relationships.

The unity for which Jesus prayed is essential among priests
and bishops. There are many subtle ways through which the

devil tries to divide the priesthood. He fosters a spirit of competition in place of mutual support and isolation in place of fraternity.

Pope John Paul II, in his first letter of 1979, said to priests and bishops, "The love for Christ and the church unites us." One of the great needs in the church is for priests to love, support, encourage, and pray for one another.

When giving retreats to priests, I always urge them to develop a strong spirit of love and fraternity. When I talk about loving, I am not talking only about saying nice things. I am talking about being a brother to a man who needs a brother, to say, "Don't do what you're going to do" or "Do what you are supposed to do."

I remember some years ago, in the north of Ireland, I was speaking to a group of priests. One priest said he was discouraged because he had just come from the funeral of a child who had been a victim of the violence. He felt torn between his desire to be a priest of the gospel and the people's demand that he be a political leader.

Seeing his great dilemma, his brother priests gathered around and prayed with him and encouraged him to do what he knew was his duty. Their love and support renewed his strength.

In any diocese, when priests are strongly united with one another and their bishop, the laity more easily develop a sense of Catholic identity. This enhances a strong Catholic, Christian voice in the secular community. Such unity also embodies the gospel character of the church, "See how those Christians love one another."

The Value of Celibacy

I would like to reflect on the value and meaning of celibacy in modern society. Today, one can hardly say the word "love" without having people immediately think of sex. When you say that celibate men and women must love, many people wonder about the church's ruling on celibacy. How can these un-married people truly love if they never know the intimacy of sexual love, if they have never experienced the love of their own children?

Many people admit that they do not understand celibacy. Celibacy is scorned. People see no value in it. They say the church imposes celibacy, that it should be optional, and that mandatory celibacy should be done away with.

Celibacy is not a denial of human love. It is not a denial of the possibility of having support from, and good friendships with, persons of the opposite sex. Celibacy does not call me to deny my sexuality and all of its attractions and emotions. Such a strained and unnatural attitude toward my own sexuality would not prepare me to be a representative of Jesus Christ who is the man of love.

Celibacy is not a denial of the beauty of fatherhood or of motherhood. It is not a denial of the need that I have for support from both men and women. It would be a lie to believe I can go through life as a minister of Jesus Christ without the love and support of other believers.

As with all commitments, celibacy is demanding and calls for discipline, self-denial, and faithfulness in prayer. Celibacy is not something to fear, not something to hinder me from being a person of love. It is a gift that enables me to love men and women into a fuller relationship with God. Celibacy is a gift and I am invited by the Lord to respond to his invitation to a celibate way of life. Celibacy is not forced upon me.

For me, as a woman, celibacy is a call to love with a power that comes through my generosity to say yes to God. That yes invites me to consecrate my womanhood and its capacities and potential to God, in a special way, for his kingdom. In doing so, I embrace a spiritual motherhood which can only be fulfilled by a life of service to others. Men called to celibacy likewise consecrate themselves to a spiritual fatherhood and life of service.

Pope John Paul II, in his first letter to priests after he became pope, had this to say about celibacy:

> The often widespread view that priestly celibacy in the Catholic Church is an institution imposed by law on those who receive the Sacrament of Orders is the result of a misunderstanding, if not downright bad faith. We all know that it is not so. Every Christian who receives the Sacrament of Orders commits himself to celibacy with full awareness and freedom after training lasting a number of years, and after profound reflection and assiduous prayer. He decides upon a life of celibacy only after he has reached a firm conviction that Christ is giving him this gift for the good of the church and the service of others. Only then does he commit himself to observe celibacy for his entire life.

The commitment to celibacy does not free us from sexual temptations. Those temptations will come just as they come in every vocation in life. I believe the devil will harass us because we are willing to accept this radical choice for the building up of the kingdom.

When I make a commitment, I have to let go of other choices. We forge our future by a commitment. A fearful or passive or indecisive person, a wavering person, ends up an unhappy person, an unfulfilled and a fragmented person. Trying to keep all options open, we realize none of them.

When I minister with priests—or with anyone else—I always tell them that they do not have to tell me their problems. They need only be aware that the Lord knows them and loves them. I just say, "Let me pray with you, Father, and I am sure that if there is anything the Lord wants to give you he will do so."

Often the Lord will give me an image—perhaps a scene from the gospel—that he knows will speak to the priest with whom I am praying. About 99 percent of the time it has something to do with the inner life of the priest. These insights in prayer are a gift from God that he gives me so his priests and people can feel his presence and love in an unmistakable, personal, and relevant way.

It is a very beautiful experience to see God touch his priests and bishops with such love and compassion.

Now, let me share with you a beautiful story, which was a great teaching for me about my own spiritual motherhood and the importance of my loving these men with a mother's heart.

On this particular occasion, I was ministering in Lourdes to a large group of priests. As usual, I was spending a lot of time in individual ministry with the bishops and priests.

One morning, I went down to the grotto to pray. As I sat there, I felt a hand on my shoulder and then I received this little kiss on my cheek. I looked up and saw this elderly priest. He sat down next to me and said, "Sister Briege, I want to thank you for being my mother."

I smiled and thought, "My, miracles never cease. Here I am 36 years of age and my son is 80!"

He said, "I didn't know you'd be here, Sister. I came down this morning to thank our Lady for sending you. My mother died when I was five. I had seven brothers and no sisters. I went into the seminary at a very early age and never had contact with women.

"To me, celibacy meant I had to keep away from women and must never allow myself to come in contact with them. I lived my whole priesthood avoiding women. So, I went through my life rejecting my sexuality, becoming a man who was very hard-hearted. Here I am at 84. I never thought I would come to a retreat that a woman was giving. Yesterday, when I went in for your ministry, I didn't know what I was going to say to you. I didn't know how to relate to women.

"As you started to talk to me, it was as though you read my whole life story with the tenderness of Jesus. As I broke down and started to cry, because I was so moved, you put your arm around me and let me cry.

"For the first time in my life, I felt the tenderness of a mother. I never knew what it was to be touched and to have a woman put her arm around me."

He said, "I never had devotion to our Lady. She was a woman and women were out of my life. Through your ministry, I

experienced the warmth and tenderness of Mary, the mother of
Jesus. I have accepted Mary as my mother. I want to thank you,
Sister."

I rejoiced at that. That is the very reason I am a celibate, that I
may be able to bring Christ to his people. There are many ways
to bring Christ, but to me, this was the most beautiful way, to
know that I introduced that priest to Mary, to the tenderness of
a mother, to the beauty of womanhood, to a part of his own life
that had not been touched.

How could he be a man of love, of tenderness, of compassion
if his own heart had never been touched by humanity?

It was the great humanity and warmth of Jesus that attracted
the crowds. We have celibates today who mirror these qualities
of Jesus. There are many, but two who come immediately to
mind are John Paul II and Mother Teresa.

I once asked Mother Teresa what she thought was the
greatest message I could give to priests. She smiled, took my
hand and said, "Sister Briege, tell them they must ask Jesus to
give them his heart to love with. Tell them they must be men of
love, that they must love the sinner, not the sin."

Celibacy is not an easy call, but it comes from the Lord
himself. We read in Matthew 19 Jesus' views on divorce and
remarriage. The disciples suggest that, if this were the case,
it would be better not to marry.

Jesus said (vv. 11-12), "Not everyone can accept this
teaching, only those to whom it has been given to do so. Some
men are incapable of sexual activity from birth; some have
deliberately been made so; and some there are who have freely
renounced sex for the sake of God's reign. Let him accept this
teaching who can."

The Fatherhood of the Priest

The priest is called to be a father. What is a father?

A father is a man who is used by God to bring life. The action
of a man in bringing physical life is only the beginning of
fatherhood. To bring a child into the world is a very small part,

but the fullness of fatherhood is realized only when a father loves, forms, corrects, and leads his children. A father must be present and show tenderness and compassion to his children. He provides his children with food so they may grow and be strong. He provides for their education. He teaches them right from wrong, gives them a moral sense, brings them up in the love and fear of God. He prepares them for society and a world in which they in turn will do the same.

That's the role of a man who physically fathers and then loves his children. The same duties are required of a priest as father of the faithful.

God has chosen the priest as a spiritual father. The first call of the priest is to love the church to whom he has committed his life. He is to love God in the church. He is to be loyal to the church. Then, as the father of the faith-family, he must teach and challenge his people. He must feed them with the word of God and the Bread of Life.

I encourage priests to develop a devotion to God the Father and ask God to let his fatherhood reflect through them.

A bishop must be a father to his priests as well as to the people. He must be the one who is not afraid to be tender when his priests are broken, not afraid to challenge when there is a need to challenge or to exercise decisive authority when necessary.

During a priests' retreat, a priest came to me for ministry, and as I was praying with him, I got a beautiful picture of Jesus. He was kneeling on a rugged road holding the priest's hands and saying to him, "Robert, forgive yourself, I have forgiven you. Come back to me. Remember the story of the prodigal son. That was you. I'm waiting for you to come back to me. Forgive yourself and return to me again."

I told him, "Father, I don't know what's wrong in your life, but the Lord has really forgiven you for the mistake you made."

The priest broke down and then he told me that he had made a terrible mistake, that he had very rashly made a decision that caused a lot of scandal. He took a leave of absence and went home to his parents. Every morning he would go into the parish church in his parents' home town and weep, telling God what a terrible mistake he had made. He felt he could never go back, that the bishop would be angry with him and would not welcome him.

One day, after a whole year, he read the story of the prodigal son in Luke 15. He got the courage to go back to see his bishop. He said, "I got on my knees and begged the bishop to forgive me and asked him to take me back.

"You know, Sister Briege, I will never forget what the bishop did. The bishop was sitting at his desk. He got up and came around the desk and took me in his arms. He said, like a father to a son, 'Robert, I'll take you back. Jesus has forgiven you and so do I. But I want you to do one thing. I want you to go to Sister Briege's retreat and I want you to come back to me after the retreat and tell me how you got on. I'll place you in a parish.'"

Robert had a tremendous experience. It totally changed his life. He came to know the mercy and love of Jesus. I think he also . experienced the tenderness and compassion and the fatherhood of his bishop. The bishop didn't condemn him or blame him for the shame he had brought on the diocese, even though it was true. Instead, he received his priest in love, as Jesus had. We need to pray that every priest and bishop will have the heart of a father, and will discern how to respond in love in any situation.

Relationships

As I reflect on the area of relationships, I am reminded of St. Clare, the foundress of our order, who loved and supported St. Francis in a truly Christ-centered relationship. Their inspired relationship with God and each other gave birth to the great spiritual family of Franciscans that has been serving the church for eight hundred years.

Some men and women, who have already made the perma-nent choice to be celibate, now say they feel that the Lord wants them to marry. I cannot easily accept that statement, but see their situation as a testing of their commitment of service in the church as people single for the Lord.

There are three lessons the Lord taught me about a relationship I have with a priest. The lessons have to do with possessiveness, reverence, and the difference between secretiveness and prudence.

First, any Christian, but especially a religious celibate, must remember he or she cannot be possessed by anyone except Jesus. Nobody can possess me. To possess or manipulate another person into bondage is wrong.

Second, I must have reverence for the other person. If God has given me a friend with whom I can speak and share my faith, I must revere that person and support his vocation.

Third, I must know the difference between prudence and secretiveness. I do not have to be afraid or secretive if I have a priest-friend with whom I can relate and share in my journey toward Christ. I have to be prudent. To be prudent is to avoid situations in which you may cause scandal or endanger your own commitment. We are all flesh and blood. The devil tries to find ways to get us to fall. It is important that I keep nothing hidden from my confessor and follow his advice.

Some years ago, I gave a talk on the priesthood to some five thousand lay people. A number of priests were in attendance also. I spoke about the beauty of the priesthood and shared much of what I have already said in this chapter.

After my talk, the lay people said they were thrilled. But several priests came up and, from what they said, I knew that they were in bad relationships. My talk had confronted them with an image of priesthood they had set aside or forgotten.

I told them they were deceiving no one but themselves, that they had made their commitment to Jesus and they were taking back their promise. I talked to them about the great dangers of hypocrisy and compromise. If I am not honest and do not try to live what I profess to be, if I am not pure and don't try to be chaste, if I don't live this single life for the Lord, I deceive myself.

As a result of this encounter with these priests, I felt the need to go away and spend time in prayer and fasting. I went to

Mother Angelica's monastery in Birmingham. During the retreat, the Lord revealed to me the many areas of priestly life for which I should pray.

One day as I prayed before the Blessed Sacrament, the Lord brought me, in my imagination, to a seminary where I saw a group of priests gathered around Jesus. The Lord turned the face of one priest toward me. He showed me this priest and he said, "Look at this priest. You will come to know him. He will teach you much about the priesthood. He will be a great protection in your life. Together you will bring many souls to me. Do not be afraid."

Immediately I thought of all the difficulties priests were experiencing. I felt secure working alone. The thought of working closely with a priest posed a threat.

Three years later, I was in Ireland and was invited to go meet a priest in Dublin at All Hallows College. He was starting the Intercession for Priests, a month-long program in which priests learn the value and power of intercession. I hesitated at first, because I was on holidays, but because of my love for the priesthood and my interest in the topic, I went to Dublin to meet Fr. Kevin Scallon.

We talked about the value of intercession and I shared with him my experience in ministry to priests. When I was leaving him, he asked me if I would come to the Intercession at some time to pray with the priests. I said I would and as I left, I kept wondering where I had seen Father Kevin before.

I heard an inner voice say, "This is the priest I showed you. You will come to know him."

At that very moment, the picture of the seminary, the whole image of three years before, was brought back to me. I suddenly realized that All Hallows Seminary was the one I had seen in this image.

As time went on, I started getting invitations to give retreats where Father Kevin had also been invited. Continually, we were brought together without any planning or effort on our part.

From our relationship over these last ten years, we have both gained a clearer understanding of the value and the richness of celibacy. We have been individually enriched by working together and sharing our commitment to be single for the Lord.

One of the great protections in this kind of team ministry is submission to our superiors. Father Kevin's provincial and my mother general are both supportive of our team ministry. We have prayed with them and sought God's guidance through them. Father Kevin and I have traveled extensively ministering to priests in such places as Africa, Europe, North and South America, Australia, and the Far East.

I want to share an experience that expresses the richness of a relationship rooted in the Lord. It had a profound effect on both Father Kevin and myself and made us very conscious of the abiding presence of Christ.

We were having dinner at a restaurant in Dublin and Father Kevin was opposite me. Calling us to prayer before our meal, he said, "Let's ask Jesus to visit us now as he did on the road to Emmaus."

At that moment, as he said those words, I bowed my head and waited for him to continue the prayer, but he didn't say anything. I looked up to see what was keeping him. And sitting in the empty seat—I am sure it was in my spirit, but I saw clearly—was a beautiful image of Jesus smiling at me. Without saying anything he transmitted to me these words, "I'm always present where I'm loved, revered, and welcomed." Then the image faded.

Father Kevin looked up at me. I could see that he was moved. He said, "I just felt someone sit beside me." His feeling confirmed what I had seen.

Should Women Be Priests?

Recognizing my ministry in the church today and the many reasons put forward that women should be ordained, I am often asked why I don't campaign for the ordination of women. I am asked if I feel inadequate or resentful because I cannot be ordained.

I respond that I've always been comfortable with the position and the teachings of the Holy Father. Because of the pain and the confusion this issue is causing in the church, I went before the Lord and asked him for a clearer understanding of his plan for the church. I asked him for courage to accept, even in the midst of opposition, my own convictions and beliefs.

In reflecting on the problem, I had often used human reasons to explain why women are not priests. I had never before really prayed about this issue or sought his wisdom.

What I learned has given me great joy. For me, it is the answer to the question. Others may disagree, but I will share it here in the event it might be of some benefit.

While praying before the Blessed Sacrament, I heard the Lord say, "Now I am going to bring you into a new awareness of the ministerial priesthood."

I saw a vision of God's plan for his church which he built on the rock, Peter. The first thing was an image of Peter and Jesus placing the big key to the church in the fisherman's hand. I became very conscious of the greatness of the church Christ had founded on Peter, of the Lord's faithfulness in giving us our present pope who is today standing as a visible sign on earth. He does not cater to people's ideas nor does he water down the plan of God or the challenges of the gospel as he understands it.

He is called to lead us in truth and to protect the truths of the church and of Christ. The mission of the church is to evangelize the world with gospel values. The world does not have a mission to evangelize the church. The first part of the vision is seeing Jesus and Peter, his Vicar.

From there I seemed to go back to creation. I saw Adam and Eve in the perfection of their humanity. As he had planned, they were made in the image and likeness of God. At this time, this voice said to me, "To be fully human is to be fully perfect. Sin is what distorts humanity." Today, people use their humanity as an excuse to sin. However, if we are fully human, as God intended, we are free from sin.

It is important to recognize that original sin came through

our first parents. In their human nature, they disobeyed God. It was not just a man and a woman, but God's choicest part of creation that broke away from him, that part that was most like him, made in the image of his Son, possessing both a physical body and a spiritual soul. The effect of that disobedience has affected each of us. We are born with that sin, since it is our nature that sinned. We receive from humanity precisely what it is.

We know from Scripture that God clearly revealed that he would use humanity, both man and woman, as key figures in his redemptive plan.

Then in my imagination, I saw Mary who was created in the most beautiful and fully human perfection, free of sin as were Adam and Eve before the fall. God was going to use a woman in the plan of redemption. She was fully human and full of the perfection of God.

The Lord could have put Jesus down on earth without woman. He's God. He could have done anything. But he chose to use woman, to come into the very womb of a human being. In doing so, I believe—and this is what came to me—at that moment God raised all womanhood to a dignity it had never known.

God visited womankind in visiting Mary. Through Adam and Eve all humanity would suffer the terrible effects of sin. Now through Mary and the fruit of her womb, all humanity would know the marvelous effects and power of redemption. We would all be affected.

In Jesus, human nature said yes overcoming Adam's no. God chose Mary to share in redemption just as Eve had shared in the fall.

I was filled with joy. I realized the full implications of God coming into the womb of a woman. God took on flesh. He was conceived of the Holy Spirit, but everything he needed for his physical body came from Mary. More than that, Mary was the one who nurtured and loved him. She did all the things that a mother is so good at doing. In what a beautiful way he honored womankind!

Then I saw Jesus walking to Calvary and being nailed to the cross. The voice said, "Oh, but death will not keep me from my people, for I have conquered sin through this death. I love my people. I will come to them."

He continued to unfold his plan to me. He said he would continue to be with us, he would give himself to us in a physical way. I recalled the Last Supper, the institution of the Eucharist. This time, the Lord would not come back to us in recognizable human form, but hidden, yet fully human and fully divine, under the appearance of bread and wine.

For his own reasons, God chose men to fulfill this part of his plan, to bring the Lord to our altars.

We cannot probe or explain God's plans. We do not know why he chose to come as a man born of a woman. We do not know why he chose only men to be priests. But the person of faith accepts that the mind of Christ and the plan of Christ will be unfolded in the church through the bishops of the world united with the Vicar of Christ.

Then, my eyes were opened to see for myself, that nobody has a right to the priesthood. It is God's gift. I do not have the right to tell God, "You give me power to bring you on the altar! You give me power to change bread and wine into your body and blood!"

I became aware that nobody, not even priests, has a right to the priesthood. God chooses. It is God's plan and his harmony and his will is what we must seek.

For me, that was the answer.

At the end of it all, I was aware of the Lord saying to me, "Remember, while the priest gives you the body and blood of Jesus in the Eucharist, it is the same body that Mary carried in her womb, brought into the world and mourned on Calvary. Mary—and therefore all of womankind—shares as intimately in the Eucharist as they do in the incarnation.

"Remember, too, that every man and woman baptized and open to the action of the Holy Spirit gives me birth as well— that where you live and work, you make me present."

Just as through Mary, Jesus entered the world, through the

priest, in the mystery of the Eucharist, Jesus comes into the church to strengthen his people for their mission in the world, that they may bring Jesus to others.

Making Jesus present in the world is the mission of all baptized Christians. We are fed with the Eucharist to enable us to do so.

I pray that what I shared with you will help us to see that our Holy Father, the Vicar of Christ, must be faithful to what he believes and knows to be the truth.

I pray that men and women of the church will rejoice in God's harmonious and creative plan for his world and for his church.

I pray that God will give us the grace to rejoice in the great things he has done for us in giving us Jesus, through Mary, through the priesthood, and through each other.

SIX

Mary, a Woman for All Seasons

IN RECENT DECADES PEOPLE HAVE FOUND it difficult to identify with Mary, the mother of Jesus. Many people thought that devotion to Mary, along with many popular devotions, was no longer relevant after the Second Vatican Council.

Still, millions of Catholics today cling to their love for the Mother of God. They do not see Mary as some sort of shadowy figure from the past, as a woman whose holiness and relationship to God and Jesus have made her inaccessible and untouchable to the rest of humanity. And, among other Christians, there is a growing appreciation for Mary and her place in our faith.

Mary is human. She was a woman of her times. Because she is the mother of Jesus, because she now is with Jesus in eternity and because she was conceived without sin, she can be known as a woman fully alive, as a woman who is, as I said in the last chapter, fully human. In fact, after the fall of Adam and Eve, with the exception of Jesus, Mary is the only human being who has achieved the heights of human excellence, the fullness of human life.

Each of us was created intentionally by God. None of us is an accident. He decided to make each of us just as surely as he decided to create Mary without sin. Her Immaculate Conception was both for Jesus and for all of us.

Can you imagine God sending his Son into a dirty vessel, into a vessel so tainted with sin that the glory of his life would be dimmed? If Mary were not free of sin, do you think Gabriel could have said, "Full of grace, the Lord is with you"? Could Mary have said, "My soul magnifies the Lord ... all generations will call me blessed"?

Her sinlessness is a vision of what we were before the fall and what we can become with the saving grace of Jesus' passion, death and resurrection.

Mary is pure and without sin, but her life began in the world, in a woman's womb. She has not lost touch with the world because she loves what her Son loves—and he loves us. When Jesus was dying on the cross, he gave her to the disciple John and he gave John to her. For nearly two thousand years, Catholics have believed that Jesus was giving all of us to Mary and Mary to all of us.

I pray that we will be more open to Jesus' great gift of his own mother, a mother who desires our salvation, a mother who participates through her love for her Son in the redemption of all humanity. This is not to say she is co-Savior with Jesus. Only Jesus saves, but through love she shared Jesus' love for us, his passion for us, his mission to us. Jesus, in his mercy, let his sinless mother participate through her heart and spirit in the redemption of humanity just as Eve had participated in its downfall. In Mary, womankind finds the greatest proof of its equality with mankind. Because of Mary, humanity need never doubt that God loves women as much as he does men.

The late Pope Paul VI wrote a beautiful exhortation called "Devotion to the Blessed Mother." In this 1974 document, Paul VI realizes that because the role and social status of women has changed dramatically in recent years many people could no longer identify with the Jewish maiden of New Testament times.

However, the pope says that "the Virgin Mary has always been proposed to the faithful of the church as an example to be imitated"—but not because of the type of humble and obscure life she led or for her socio-cultural background.

She is an example to the faithful rather for the way in which, in her own particular life, she fully and responsibly accepted the will of God (cf. Lk 1:38), because she heard the word of God and acted on it, and because charity and a spirit of service were the driving force of her actions. She is worthy of imitation because she was the first and the most perfect of Christ's disciples. All of this has a permanent and universal exemplary value (nos. 34-35).

The Irish people have always had great devotion to Mary, and as a child I have memories of praying the family rosary and of revering the Mother of God. I continued my devotion to Mary all through my novitiate in the Poor Clares and all through my suffering and healing. When I was struggling with the decision to accept the gift of healing, I prayed and begged Mary to intercede for me, to keep me in the heart of the church, and to help me respond to whatever it was God wanted of me.

I will share some experiences that show how, even in the present day, this great woman continues to echo her Cana message (Jn 2:5), pointing to her Son and saying, "Do whatever he tells you." This is her role in the church: to call her children continually to respond to God's will and to be obedient to the voice of God.

Shortly after I had accepted the gift of healing, I had the privilege of going to Lourdes. While I was in Lourdes, I was sitting in front of the grotto, watching as the sick were being brought to the area for intercession. I was touched by the whole scene and the realization of how closely Mary is involved in the healing ministry of Christ. As I looked on, in my spirit I heard, "Because of your love for my mother, you too will share in her work here at Lourdes."

I thought, "Wouldn't it be beautiful to be able to pray with people here at Lourdes." But I thought it was impossible since I was there only as a pilgrim.

I left the grotto and went to the chapel where the Blessed

Sacrament was exposed. The voice said again, "Because of your love for my mother, you too will share in her work here at Lourdes."

Less than an hour later, while I was in a cafe having coffee with a couple from Florida, my eyes were drawn to a priest walking down the street. He had a name tag which identified him as coming from the diocese of Armagh, my home diocese.

I greeted him and told him I was from the Armagh diocese but now living in Florida. He said, "Are you Sister Briege McKenna?" When I said I was he asked, "Would you do me a favor? There are four hundred invalids down in the hospital from your home district. Would you come down and pray with them?"

I went with him. As I walked from bed to bed, nearly all of them said they had written to me in Florida asking me to pray for them. In their letters they asked whether I would be returning to Ireland soon so that I might pray with them personally. I wasn't planning to go to Ireland, but the Lord brought this part of Ireland to Lourdes at the same time I was there.

As I prayed with these people, I realized the Lord was fulfilling what he had told me, that I was sharing in his mother's ministry at Lourdes. I knew I was experiencing the real miracles that take place at Lourdes other than physical healing: the grace to be filled with joy even in the midst of suffering, and to accept suffering in a spirit of reparation and intercession.

Since that first experience, I have ministered several times in Lourdes, but the highlights of my ministry there were the times I was invited to participate in giving priests' retreats. One of those retreats was attended by many priests who were ill. These priests were brought into the lecture hall in their sick beds. It was inspiring to see them singing God's praises as I walked from bed to bed praying with them. On one retreat, which I shared with a French priest, we had more than five hundred priests attending.

Worldwide Mission

In Tampa in 1973, I had a dream which, at the time, didn't make sense to me. Later, as the dream became a reality, I realized it had been a prophetic dream.

In the early morning of January 1, 1973, I dreamed that I was in the chapel before a statue of Mary and she had a globe in her hand. As I looked up at her, I was thinking how beautiful she was, when she looked at me and smiled.

I looked and thought, in the dream, "Oh, she's alive." Then she bent down and gave me the globe. As I took the globe, she whispered in my ear. I told her I would never forget what she said.

I turned, in the dream, to walk out of the chapel. As I did so I heard a phone ringing. I woke up and my phone was indeed ringing. It was about four in the morning, and I was half asleep when I answered. It was a priest who apologized for calling so early but said that his mother was dying and wanted my prayers. I prayed with him.

I tried to remember the details of the dream but could not. I couldn't remember what she had said to me. I went back to sleep—and dreamed the same dream again!

I went back to the same chapel. Everything happened as it did the first time. She whispered in my ear and I again told her I would never forget what she said. As I walked out of the chapel, still in the dream, some people came running up to me. It had not fully registered with me that this was indeed Mary, but these people in the second dream asked, "What did Mary say to you?"

I said, "I don't know, I've forgotten." I got frustrated with myself. How could I forget so soon? I had just left her. In the dream, I then saw a sister who had been in the novitiate with me. She came up to me and said, "Oh, Briege, I know what our Lady told you. She said she gave a message to your spirit and when the time comes, you will remember it but it is not for now."

She said, "The globe she gave you is the universe that you will travel."

Then I woke up. I would later understand how prophetic this dream really was since I was doing very little travelling at that time.

Miracles in Brazil

Several years later, on the four hundredth anniversary of St. Vincent de Paul, Father Kevin got a prompting of the Spirit to enroll me in the Association of the Miraculous Medal.

Our Lady said that those who wear this medal with confidence will be blessed, but the medal is not like a good luck charm. As a pamphlet on the medal says, it is "a little token of love designed and bestowed upon you by the Blessed Virgin." People wear the medal as a reminder of their faith in God and in Mary's power as an intercessor with her Son.

Where does this medal come from? On November 27, 1830, the Blessed Mother appeared to Sister Catherine Laboure in the chapel of the motherhouse of the Daughters of Charity on the Rue du Bac in Paris. Sister Catherine described the Blessed Mother as "beautiful in the perfection of her beauty."

When Mary appeared as she is on the medal, Sister Catherine heard the words, "Have a medal struck on this model. All who wear it will receive great graces."

In a previous visit, our Lady had said, "Come to the foot of the altar. Here graces will be bestowed." From Mary, Sister Catherine learned how to pray. Later, Catherine was herself declared a saint.

Father Kevin talked to me about the value of distributing the medal. Giving me five hundred medals, he suggested that I distribute them during my upcoming visit to Brazil, where I had been invited by then President Figueiredo.

A few days before I left for Brazil, I had word that the president was very ill. He had had a serious heart attack. I left for Brazil on October 7. When I arrived at the president's residence, he was surrounded by doctors and state officials.

Within a few days, he was to be flown to the United States for open-heart surgery.

I prayed with him, and while praying a prompting came to me to give him a miraculous medal. I did so and told him the story. I was surprised at his joy. He asked, "Has anyone told you what I have just done?"

More than 200,000 people were gathered at the shrine of Our Lady of Aparecida. Many of the bishops concelebrated the mass that day. The vice president led the act of consecration in the absence of President Figueiredo. He said the shrine was personally important to him since he had chosen to be married there twenty-five years before. He offered a moving prayer, from the heart, in which he asked Mary to intercede with her Son for the church and for the government. He prayed that justice might prevail throughout the nation and that the teaching of Pope John Paul II might be implemented.

President Figueiredo told me that as soon as he had come into office he declared a national holiday in honor of Mary, October 12, the feast of Our Lady of Aparecida—in spite of opposition from spiritists and Christians who did not understand the role of Mary. I left the president that day and at his invitation went to pray with the various members of his cabinet and other national officials. As I prayed with the leaders of the country, I was aware of our Lady's presence. I pinned the medal on each of them and received a word from the Lord for each one. It was as though the Lord showed me their inner lives. They were profoundly touched.

The president went to America for surgery. He had resisted the trip at first because he feared surgery. As it was, doctors had told him he would be convalescing for at least sixty days.

However, the doctors in Cleveland said he did not need immediate surgery, so he returned home. While he did have surgery nearly two years later, the president experienced a tremendous spiritual healing—and God's power was manifested in several personal instances in his family. As a Christmas present that year, he gave each member of his family a medal.

I was overwhelmed at the faith and devotion of the Brazilian

Catholics. As a result of one of my talks, the country's leading ladies organized a eucharistic procession and a rosary crusade for peace in the country and in the world. The event took place in Brasilia, the nation's capital.

When I came home to Tampa and reflected on this visit to Brazil, I was moved by the many conversions and healings that had taken place. Many said, when I gave them this little medal, a token of Mary, that they felt an urge to return to the practice of their faith. Others reported physical healings and many healings of relationships.

Our Lady has said that those who wear this medal with confidence will be blessed—but the medal is not a good luck charm. In fact, the church has been clear in her regard of the medal. As a pamphlet on the medal states, it is a "little token of love designed and bestowed upon you by the Blessed Virgin."

People wear the medal as a reminder of their faith in God and their understanding of Mary's power as an intercessor with her Son.

The medal was given to Sister Catherine Laboure, on November 27, 1830, in Rue-du-bac, the chapel of the motherhouse of the Daughters of Charity in Paris. Mary appeared to Sister Catherine as she appears in the image on the medal, and told her, "Have a medal struck on this model. All who wear it will receive great graces."

Later, Sister Catherine herself was declared a saint.

About two months after my return to Tampa, I was in the chapel in my usual time of prayer when I heard clearly, "Briege, you must go to the Rue du Bac."

I wasn't going to Paris and didn't see how I could go to the Rue du Bac. In March, I was supposed to go to Belgium to visit Cardinal Suenens, but Belgium isn't Paris. Still, the thought became very strong, "You will go."

Three days later, Mrs. Margie Grace from New York phoned me. She and her husband, Peter, have been very supportive of my ministry. Margie knew I was going overseas to Europe and she said that their plane was going to Europe and offered me a ride. She asked me where I would be going. I told her that I was going to Belgium, but I had a real desire to go to Paris to visit the Rue du Bac. I arrived at the Rue du Bac on March 19, the feast of St. Joseph.

I couldn't explain the excitement and enthusiasm I felt in my spirit as I approached the Rue du Bac.

As I knelt in this beautiful little chapel, I saw this statue of Mary with a little globe in her hands. It all seemed so familiar to me. I wondered where I had seen this statue before. Suddenly, I relived my dream of 1973 and saw myself receiving the globe.

As I received the globe, a scroll unrolled before me. Written on it was, "Go and make me queen in the hearts of the people you meet. Tell the world of my motherly love and protection. This globe is the world you will travel. As I become queen of my people, I will be queen of the world. And there will be peace." I realized that this was the message I couldn't remember from my dream.

Then I had an image of a lifeless and withered human heart. Our Lady showed me a key which she inserted into the heart. Opening the heart, she placed something within it and the heart was suddenly vibrantly alive.

She said I should use the miraculous medal as means of introducing her to people. She, in turn, would bring them to her Son, Jesus, who gives us life. Now I understood why in Brazil so many people to whom I gave the medal were open to the life-giving power of Jesus.

Three days later, without knowing about this experience, a friend gave me a miraculous medal in the shape of a key.

Since that time I have traveled over the world with thousands of medals. More than that, I have begun to see a new dimension in the healing ministry: people returning to our Catholic faith, people returning to the sacrament of reconciliation.

The Queen of Peace

At the Rue du Bac, our Lady told me she would be known as the Queen of Peace. Some years later, many people believe that Mary began appearing at Medjugorje, Yugoslavia, in which she strongly urged people to repent and to pray for peace.

In May of 1981, I was ministering in Rome and I had the privilege of praying with Fr. Tomislav Vlasic, a priest from Medjugorje. He had asked me to pray for his parish ministry back in Yugoslavia. I received one of the images I often get. I saw a white church with twin steeples. Father was sitting in the main celebrant's chair in the sanctuary of this church and streams of living water were flowing from the altar. Many people were coming and cupping the water in their hands to drink of this water.

Father Tomislav was very consoled by this image because his parish was going through hard times. The church was experiencing great difficulties. The government was less than sympathetic toward the church.

It was about a month later, on June 24, that our Lady made her first appearance to the five youths of Medjugorje. She has been appearing daily since that time and there have been many conversions and miracles in that rural Yugoslavian village. Thousands of people come from all over the world.

Mary is asking people to return to her Son and telling them that if they would pray, fast, and go to confession, there would be many conversions and conversions would lead to peace. Again, she called herself the Queen of Peace. Father Tomislav found himself in the very church I had described to him in the image in Rome.

As the interest in Medjugorje grew, people asked me whether I would go there. Even though many people were surprised that I had no plans to go to Medjugorje, I had never felt led or prompted to go.

In March of 1985, I was giving a retreat in Ireland. While giving this retreat, I met an Irish gentleman who is now living in England. He showed great surprise that I had not been to Medjugorje and seemed sure that I would eventually go. He even offered to make all the arrangements and promised that he and his wife would accompany me if I decided to go.

I thanked him for his offer, but responded that my schedule

was very full over the next year or two and that I didn't foresee any opportunity to go. He left that afternoon and would return to England the next morning.

Early next morning while praying the rosary, I got an overwhelming sense of Mary's presence and seemed to hear a voice say, "You must go to Medjugorje and there I will give you a message for my priests. You will go on the Feast of Corpus Christi."

Wondering if it was just my imagination or a longing in me, after hearing so much about Medjugorje, I prayed for guidance and discernment. Three things came to me that seemed to confirm the message.

I opened the Scriptures to the passage that I had received for Father Tomislav in 1981 about the living waters. Second, the only week and a half I had free during the next year was the week in June in which Corpus Christi fell. Third, I knew that because of my vows, I would have to submit the idea to my mother general. Her response would also confirm if I should go. Her response was very enthusiastic.

Another confirmation came when the gentleman from England returned. He had been ready to leave and got a strong urge to return to the retreat center where I was giving the retreat.

So I went to Medjugorje. During his homily at mass the first night I was there, Fr. Tomislav Pervan spoke with great enthusiasm and power to a packed church. As he preached, I began to cry even though I couldn't understand what he was saying in Croatian. But I was getting an image of a group of priests being overcome by evil and sin. They didn't believe in the power they had to overcome sin. It was a sad and frightening scene.

After the mass was over, I asked Father what he had preached about. His sermon corresponded to my image. He had preached about sin in the world and the need to call on the power of Christ, the need to clothe oneself with the armor of Christ (Eph 6:10-17). He talked about the priesthood and the importance of confronting the forces of evil.

I did get a message from Mary which I share with the priests when I give retreats. I also had an opportunity to minister to the prayer groups and to the young people there and to be in the room of the apparitions. I spoke with the visionaries.

Young people today are exploited by society and attacked by Satan. To be pure and chaste is not accepted by society. But in Medjugorje, I witnessed a tremendous sense of Mary's presence and her purity in the young people, particularly in those who belong to the prayer group our Lady told the visionaries to organize.

In my ministry to this prayer group, I told them about remaining faithful to the quest for holiness. I told them to be aware at all times of the efforts of the Evil One to deter them from holiness. I shared with them the joy of giving one's life to Jesus and said that God will never be outdone in generosity. The next day, Jelana, one of the visionaries, received a message from our Lady which confirmed my teaching.

I've celebrated Corpus Christi all my life as a special day, but nowhere have I celebrated it surrounded by such faith, reverence, and love for the Eucharist as in Medjugorje.

Mary has taught me so many beautiful things about bringing people to her Son. One of the ways is the rosary. Padre Pio, the saintly mystic, said of the rosary: "Mary put a sword into the hands of her children, and that sword is the rosary."

I believe the rosary is simply walking with Mary through the life of Jesus.

Pope Paul VI talked about the rosary as a "Gospel Prayer, centered on the mysteries of the redemptive incarnation. The Rosary is a prayer with a clearly Christological orientation."

As a Sister of St. Clare, I believe with all my sisters around the world that we must be inspired by a great love for Mary, the Virgin Mother, seeing our life of celibacy as a source of spiritual fruitfulness in the church and prophetic sign to all people of God of the future life of glory which awaits them in the resurrection.

SEVEN

Let's Go—In the Name of the Lord!

A S I LEFT HOME and embraced the life of a Poor Clare, it would have been inconceivable to think or imagine the plan the Lord had for my life. His plans would take me far from my homeland to the ends of the earth to proclaim his gospel.

St. Clare, the foundress of our congregation, once received a word from God for St. Francis, which as a Franciscan, I also take to heart:

God did not call you for yourself alone
but also for the salvation of others.

I recognize, because of our Franciscan freedom, we are enabled, with the liberty so characteristic of the spirit of Clare, to express joyfully our charisms in diverse apostolates.

It is with joy and the blessing and support of my congregation that I go, in the name of the Lord, to proclaim his love and his healing power. Through my travels, God has enriched my life and filled it with praise for his goodness and love for mankind.

It is the Lord who does wonders. I am convinced through his goodness that no one can do more than become a signpost that points to him, to help others discover him in their hearts and permit him to give them great blessings.

I have traveled, as our Lady said, all over the globe. In these recent years, a new dimension has also come to my international travels since meeting Father Kevin. He has a great love for the Eucharist, as I have, and a great awareness of its power.

We witnessed this eucharistic power on a recent visit to the Far East. Father Kevin walked down the aisles of a stadium filled with more than twenty thousand people. We had given them a teaching on the Jesus who really loves them and is truly present in the Eucharist. Father Kevin asked them to raise up their hands toward the monstrance containing the sacred Host, and to ask Jesus to bless them and heal them.

I stood at the microphone praying, and encouraging them to focus their attention and faith on the Lord. This is where the focus should be. There is always danger of people looking to a minister instead of to the Lord.

In Taiwan, a country in which so many people turn to false gods, we proclaimed the gospel to many nonbelievers. But we also saw a need for Catholics to discover the great power of the Eucharist and the other gifts our faith gives us.

We emphasized the sacraments, particularly the sacrament of reconciliation. The anointing of the sick brought many marvelous miracles of healing.

In the Far East we saw many non-Christians fall on their knees before the sacred Host and acknowledge that this was Jesus. Later, they would ask us to explain to them our faith and the mystery of the Eucharist.

A very beautiful experience in Hawaii shows the great and indiscriminate love of Jesus. In one of our healing services, Father Kevin walked down the aisle processing with the Blessed Sacrament. I stood at the microphone praying for healing as they focused on Jesus. A young Catholic woman had brought a Mormon friend with her. The Mormon girl had deformed hands. They had hoped we would pray with the girl. To their great surprise we were not praying individually with people, but we brought Jesus among them and told them to focus on him.

Just as in Lourdes, Father held up the monstrance and blessed the people. The young Mormon girl explained later that she did not really understand our teaching on the Eucharist, but realized that we Catholics thought this Host was the real presence of Jesus.

Looking at the sacred Host as Father Kevin blessed the people, she asked Jesus to ease the pain of her deformed hands. As she looked at the Host, she felt something come from it and go through her body. As she walked out of the church, she nudged her Catholic friend and said, "Look." She held out her hands and they were healed.

Miracles do happen! We believe that the Lord, as much as he was doing for that Mormon girl, was also saying to us Catholics, "Do you see and believe in my power?"

Ministry in South America

South America has become a very familiar territory to me. I have spent many months traveling in many countries such as Chile, Peru, Brazil, and Venezuela. In 1979, I had a memorable mission to Latin America.

I encountered my first earthquake in a place called Vina del Mar in Chile. While it caused little damage, it frightened me to find my bed doing a little jig around the room.

It was on this visit that God led me to a church where a priest was waiting for me. He had had a dream in which he was told to wait in this church for someone. I was the one who was also prompted to come to that church, where I was able to minister to him.

Long drives and long roads in Peru made me feel the many hazards of missionary life, but the joy and faith of the thousands who came to worship Jesus and seek his healing was very refreshing. I witnessed many healings among God's poor.

For hours, I stood and prayed with people individually.

I often heard people talk about being light-headed. It can have many meanings, but Bolivia gave me a light head—the city of La Paz is 14,500 feet above sea level. I was only passing through this city on my way to give a retreat in Cochibamba, but the course of events changed my plans. A military coup had taken place during the night.

When I arrived at the airport to leave the city, it was closed down. For the next seven days, with my Chilean interpreter, Blanca, and my American traveling companion, Jill, I lived through a frightening, bloody civil war. Each day we watched from our apartment window as soldiers shot at each other and the city was in turmoil.

After days of listening to reports that we would be unable to get out for maybe weeks, we decided to make an all-night vigil and seek God's protection. It came to us that we must not be preoccupied with ourselves, but intercede for the many poor people who were suffering as a result of this war. We felt Jesus calling us to greater trust and security in his protection. As he spoke these words, we recalled Psalm 91 which speaks of security in his protection.

Back in the United States word was out about our dilemma. Many people started to pray for our safety, but Mother Angelica, in Birmingham, is a woman who believes in action as well as prayer.

She called the State Department in Washington and reported that we were unable to get out of this dangerous zone. It worked. Two days later, we had a visit from a woman from the United States Embassy. She told us to be at the airport early the next morning. Two military planes were sent from Panama to evacuate United States citizens.

Jill and I made ourselves known to American officials at the airport. As they read down the list of names of people who were to leave the country, I smiled as the pilot asked us, "Are you the two U.S. missionaries?" I had never before thought of myself as a U.S. missionary.

What a sense of relief we felt as we boarded that military plane which flew us back to Peru. We were met by people from the American Embassy in Lima and plenty of television cameras. We were told of all that was available for United States citizens, such as planes going back home, hotels where we could stay, and many other things the Embassy was able to help us with in this emergency.

We were met by Fr. Mike LaFay, who just the week before made me promise I would return some day to Lima. He said he hadn't expected me to fulfill my promise so soon. Then, I was off to Brazil, a country I would grow to love and visit many times.

Brazilian people remind me of the Irish. I think it is the simple faith and the warm friendly manner they have. I felt very much at home in this country, in spite of the many inconveniences and the various climate changes.

Ingrid and Peter Orglmeister had planned a full schedule for my visit to Brazil. Ingrid was my interpreter in Brazil. In fact, she has traveled with me extensively throughout the world assisting me in communicating the Lord's message. She and Peter are a fine Catholic couple and have served the church in many ways.

I spoke in many places throughout Brazil. Thousands filled stadiums. On one occasion, I had to get up on a truck and from there speak to the multitude which had grown to over twenty thousand.

It was at such gatherings that I called the people to pray for priests. We would always have a mass. I would help the people focus their attention on our Lord in the Eucharist instead of on me or on themselves. I would call the priests up before mass and have the people join in prayer for them. This was a great source of encouragement to the priests who I discovered needed to be recognized and shown gratitude for their mission.

This tour of South America in 1979 was the beginning of a mission also to the priests and bishops throughout Latin America, especially Brazil. Since that visit, I have now returned to give several diocesan retreats at the invitation of the various cardinals and bishops.

Meetings with National Leaders

I've experienced the pain and struggle that missionaries feel as they try to aid the poor and cope with the oppression. In both Peru and Brazil, the Lord also gave me the opportunity to speak and pray with the presidents and officials of these countries.

A few years ago, I was sitting in a church in Lima. I sensed God asking me if I would go where he sent me and say what he told me. I was pleading with him to use me to help his people and to protect me from becoming blind to my mission to all God's people—rich and poor, oppressed and oppressor.

Later that morning, a sister suggested it would be a great idea for me to meet the president of Peru. Immediately I felt that God, that very morning, had been preparing me for a meeting with the president. At three o'clock that day, I was with the president of Peru; after a very pleasant visit, I felt Jesus telling me to pray with him.

I suggested to him that we should pray and he was delighted. As I prayed, I received an image which spoke very powerfully to this leader. I felt God's love and care for him, and I know he felt it. On that same day, I prayed with the minister of the interior and many other people. I gave away hundreds of Miraculous Medals.

Before my next trip to Brazil, in February of 1980, my father died unexpectedly. It was a very sad moment for all of us. Because of the change in schedule and the need to be with my family, I was unable to prepare adequately for a month of ministry to priests and laity. On my way to Brazil, since I felt I was so unprepared, I asked Jesus to accept my emptiness and the suffering caused by my father's death.

In spite of my lack of preparation, I felt this was one of my most powerful missions, because I had nothing of my own. Out of my poverty, I had to let the Lord work.

While traveling in Brazil, I was thinking of the many people I had met who told me of their great anger toward the government. I had also met many who felt the government was not at fault for the problems in the country. But everyone was deeply concerned about injustices in the country.

With all these thoughts, I found myself saying, "Jesus, I'd like to meet the leader of this great country. He must know you. I'd love to tell him about your love for him."

A voice answered, "You will meet the president. I will allow you to see his heart."

At that time, I had never met the president. Ingrid asked me if she should write a letter to him to make arrangements for a visit. Somehow, I felt that would not be necessary. God showed us he is always ahead of us. He only needs willing instruments and he can accomplish much more than we expect.

When we arrived in the airport in Brasilia, on our way to give a priests' retreat, the man who met us mentioned that there had been a call from the president asking if it were possible for him to meet with me.

I met President Figueiredo the next day. It was a very blessed meeting. We talked about many things and prayed. He invited Ingrid and myself to stay for supper. In the president, I saw a man who needed, as we all do, to know how much Jesus loved him and to hear the good news.

He was very moved as I prayed with him and his wife. Ingrid's remark to me later was, "I never thought you were used to talking to leaders." I think she was surprised that I freely witnessed about Jesus to the president, sharing what Jesus asked of him as a leader.

What I felt at this first meeting with President Figueiredo was an extraordinary sense of the indwelling presence of Jesus. I felt Jesus was speaking to one of his children and I was somehow just sitting there listening.

A week later I received a personal invitation from the president to return to minister to his family and other people. I did return to spend a week with many of the officials of this great land. It was on this visit that the president was sick and that the country was consecrated to Mary. I learned from this experience that we cannot "choose sinners." We cannot neglect the poor; nor can we neglect the rich; we cannot neglect commoners; nor can we neglect political leaders or people in the military. All are God's children. All must hear his word.

It would be impossible to tell you all the wonders of this one trip alone, but a few of the remarkable happenings should be shared.

First, I met again with the president and with many of the ministers. As I prayed with each one, God touched them. The minister of defense sent out an invitation to all military personnel to attend a talk given by an Irish-American sister. It was quite something to have the chance to proclaim God's word to all these military men.

I had prayed for hours before to learn what the Lord would have me say to them. Some of the wives of the men were in the charismatic renewal. No sooner had I ended the talk than they began to sing, "Our God Reigns." It was probably the first time in a big military arena that "Our God Reigns" had been sung by a thousand military men.

The governor of the federal district, Brasilia, invited me to address some top business people, politicians, and government officials. I was also given time to proclaim the gospel on midday, prime-time television.

During this trip to Brazil the president asked me to pray for his household. Of course, I thought that must be the maids and servants, but as we drove to the president's residence and got out of the car, I watched as the soldiers came marching towards where Ingrid and I stood. I was admiring them and wondering where they were off to. So I asked Ingrid, only to find out they were lining up for me to pray with them.

I thought, "No, this couldn't be possible! All these soldiers!"

The general had his soldiers line up in front of us. When they were in formation, the general saluted and then introduced me to these men. I wish I could remember that introduction, but my mind was racing and I was thinking, "What could I possibly say to all of these men?"

Then I heard in my spirit, "Give me your hands to touch and bless and transmit my healing love to them and I will give you my heart to love them."

I spoke to them about Jesus, and then I walked from soldier to soldier praying with them. Since I couldn't lay my hand on their heads because of their helmets, I put it on their hearts. I told Ingrid I had never felt so many men's thumping hearts as on that day.

Under these helmets, God showed me men he had died for. As I walked from man to man, the Lord taught me how easily we can allow a uniform to keep us from hearing what Jesus says about the greatest commandment: to love all men, and to forgive.

I saw the face of Jesus as I looked at these men. Often their eyes filled with tears. I have no doubt that as I felt the presence of Jesus they did also.

The Lord has shown me how true are the words the angel spoke to Mary at the annunciation, "Nothing is impossible with God." My response, like Mary's, must be to say yes and to believe God's words will come to pass.

Today, as I look back at the many countries in which God has allowed me to minister, I realize that Jesus is alive and active and only needs us to believe and to be ready to say, "Let's go—in the name of the Lord!"

EIGHT

Celebrate Faith with Faithfulness

B EING A CHRISTIAN means you have made a commitment to
follow Jesus Christ, to live according to his teachings and
to obey his commandments. Today, throughout the world, we
are experiencing a renewal of faith. People are accepting Jesus
for the first time or they are renewing faith in him and their
commitment to him.

As Catholics, we enjoy the fullness of revelation in Scripture.
We also believe that the Lord speaks to his people through our
history of belief, our history of falling and rising. We believe
Jesus meant what he said when he promised us that he would be
with us always and that hell would not have victory over us. We
believe Jesus meant what he said when he gave the keys of the
kingdom to Peter. We believe he meant what he said when he
told Peter to feed and tend his lambs and sheep, when he told
his apostles that what they bound and loosed would be ratified
in heaven.

We believe, in a word, that Jesus speaks to us through
tradition as well as through Scripture, that his life cannot be
contained only in the historical, although divinely inspired,
pages of the Bible; that through his Spirit, he speaks to his
church through Peter and the apostles. We believe that the
Lord speaks through the successors of Peter and the apostles.

The apostles and their successors, our tradition and our Scriptures, have taught us that the Lord gives his church specific ways in which we effect his presence among us. These are the sacraments: baptism, penance, Eucharist, confirmation, matrimony, holy orders, and anointing of the sick. The sacraments are living encounters with Jesus who strengthens us and helps us live out our commitment.

We enter into the life of God through faith. We believe that faith is a gift, freely given and celebrated in baptism. At baptism, we are adopted by the Father. On our behalf, our parents and godparents promise to help and nurture the faith. A candle symbolizing the light of Christ is given to us. We begin our journey as Christians. Baptism makes us different from the non-Christians. Now we must act and live according to the teachings and commandments of Jesus Christ.

Jesus calls us to follow him without reservation in all our work and relationships. He came to teach us how to live and act in this world. When Jesus called the apostles to follow him, his call was radical: "Come follow me." During the three years of his ministry, they came to know him personally. They must have rejoiced at all he could do—he could heal and perform miracles, and he could give hope to everybody who truly listened to him. He was a man of power. In their minds they must have thought, "What a great life we will have. Our leader is so powerful. No more problems. He has all the answers."

Yes, Jesus has all the answers, and he can do all things and he is strong, but he was going to challenge these men. They seemed to miss a point Jesus made early in his ministry: he had no place to lay his head. He had nothing that the world would value as security. He had only his Father.

One day as he spoke about his journey to Jerusalem and how he would suffer, Peter, who loved him, was horrified and tried to persuade Jesus not to go. It is as if Peter said, "You can't suffer. After all, suffering depicts weakness."

It was then that Jesus reprimanded Peter and explained to the disciples what it would mean to be his followers. The commitment they had accepted to follow him would not be easy. Jesus spoke to them in demanding words. As his followers, they must be willing to deny themselves, take up their cross, and follow him.

Jesus then proceeded to do with his own life what he challenged his apostles and followers to do. He showed total commitment to fulfill his Father's will by death on the cross.

The apostles would come to understand what Jesus was speaking about after his death and resurrection. They would understand what he meant when he said the world would hate them because the world hated him (Jn 15:18).

Jesus did not expect the apostles to live out this commitment on their own strength. He promised to send them the Spirit; we know the effects of Pentecost on his followers' lives. Their fear was transformed into a fiery faith, their sadness into joy, their despair into hope (Acts 2).

Every Christian is called to make a personal commitment to Jesus. While we express our commitment in different vocations, Jesus must be first in all of our lives. His teachings must guide our actions. His commandments must be our road signs on the journey—for clergy, religious, and laity alike.

I must never allow the world to evangelize me, so that I forget God's power and wisdom and look to worldly power and wisdom. Jesus gives us the church, our guiding light on our journey. He gives us the Vicar of Christ, the pope, and the bishops, whose mission it is to urge us continually on the journey to God. The pope and bishops must themselves remain faithful to their pastoral commitment to the church and to the gospel.

My Commitment to Jesus

As a sister of St. Clare, I made a commitment to Jesus. I now see three areas in my life through which I can learn from him how to live more fully my commitment: trust and abandonment, the cross, and victory and resurrection.

When I first made my commitment to Jesus in my religious life, I publicly committed my life to faithfulness and to trust in Jesus in whatever he would ask of me. I knelt before the bishop and my mother general and, with my hands symbolically bound, I vowed to live a life of poverty, chastity, and obedience. I signed a document saying I would be faithful for life, in much the same way married people publicly commit themselves to God and one another on their wedding day.

It was very easy to kneel there before the bishop. Those words were beautiful and inspiring. At sixteen years of age, when I took my first vows, it all seemed so definite. At twenty-one, when I received my ring symbolizing a total and perpetual commitment in the Congregation of the Sisters of St. Clare, it was great.

Now, twenty-five years after my first vows, the Lord has taught me much more about commitment. It is not saying the words that fulfills my promise, but it is the living out of it, the decisions for Jesus that I must make every day of my life.

Many people say, years after such a commitment—to religious life or marriage—that when they made their vows, they "really didn't know what was ahead" and therefore "Jesus surely can't expect me to live up to that vow."

I believe you grow in a commitment. We make the decision. We accept the invitation. The Lord promises to give us strength. Just as with the apostles, he doesn't tell us we will have an easy life. In fact, he tells us that even if we leave everything for him (Mk 10:29-30), we will suffer persecution besides. And that's not all. He says we are blessed when we suffer such persecution (Mt 5:11-12) and that we should rejoice.

So, too, with the commitment to the Sisters of St. Clare. Looking back now, I realize that commitment is not easy. There are moments in my life when I ask myself, "What have I said? What have I done?" It is at those moments that I realize the Lord gives me the grace and strength when I call on him, to be faithful to my commitment.

It was in a moment like this that I was confronted with the basic question of Christian commitment, "Who is first in your life?"

Who Is First?

My Auntie Lizzie was very dear to me, very much like a mother. In fact, before my mother died, she had asked Auntie Lizzie to look after me if anything should happen to her before I grew up.

While I didn't go to live with Auntie Lizzie in the years that followed my mother's death, I became very close to her. She became to me what a mother would be. She loved me like a daughter and was always praying for me.

As with most religious congregations, the Order of St. Clare permits sisters to visit their families, especially in times of serious illness or death. When I decided to volunteer for America, since I was so close to Auntie Lizzie and my own mother was dead, I asked my mother general whether I would be permitted to come home in the event my aunt was very ill or dying. Of course, I was given permission, and I used to say to Auntie Lizzie, "Don't you die before I come home."

She'd answer me, "I have no notion of dying. I'll be here when you come home."

In 1984 I went to Latin America. That was the trip in which we were trapped in a civil war in Bolivia. After leaving Bolivia we came to Brazil where I was to spend several weeks ministering to priests, sisters, and laity.

Within the first few days I was in Brazil, I got an early morning phone call telling me my aunt had had a stroke and was dying. I was told I should return to Ireland immediately. My superior in Tampa told me that she would get me a ticket from Tampa to Ireland and that I should come to Tampa as soon as possible.

I was terribly upset. Auntie Lizzie was very dear to me. It was almost time for mass, so I decided to wait until after mass to make arrangements to leave for Tampa. In my heart, I thought I would be able to see Auntie Lizzie before she died and that was a source of some consolation. Ingrid and Jill went to mass with me, offering me support in my grief.

During the first part of the mass, I prayed for Auntie Lizzie and thought about all I had to do before I left: my schedule was so full, some things would have to be cancelled. I had every intention of going home, because it seemed the right thing to do. I had permission, and my family expected me to come.

During the first part of the mass, I prayed for my aunt and thought about the plans, realizing that I would have to alter my schedule for the next couple of weeks.

On my way up to receive communion, all this was very much on my mind. As I put my hand out to receive the sacred Host, the Lord asked, "Briege, who is first in your life?"

I answered immediately, "You are, Jesus."

The word that came back to me very powerfully was, "Then I don't want you to go home. I brought you here. This is where you should be."

I got on the defensive and said, "Oh, but Jesus, I have to go home because my aunt is dying and I'll never see her again and I promised to go and I have permission from my mother general." I made all the excuses I could think of.

It was as though I heard the Lord repeating the words again, "Briege, who is first in your life?"

Again, I said, "You are, Jesus."

He responded, "Well then, I do not want you to go home."

At that moment I saw myself standing before the Lord, looking at him and then looking at my family. It was probably the first time, after all these years, that I really had to make the choice I had promised to make when I took my vows.

I had permission of my superior; I was expected to return home. It was the acceptable thing to do. Yet now, Jesus was putting me to the test. Where was my commitment?

There are times in all of our lives we must be willing to die to even the good desires, for the sake of the Lord's will, for what is better in his sight.

I looked at Jesus in this image after communion and I said, "Jesus, I won't go. I'll stay here." Suddenly I realized that, in a way, I had been selfish. I hadn't been thinking of Auntie Lizzie, but of myself, of my need to see her alive just once more. I was not thinking of the thousands of people all through Brazil who had arranged their schedules to host me, to hear me, to be with me in this ministry.

As soon as I submitted to Jesus, a peace came into my spirit and also a great joy—so much so that, as we were walking out of church, Ingrid and Jill remarked on how joyful I looked.

As I look back on that joy, which I could not explain at the time, I understand how Mary must have felt when she was asked to be the mother of Jesus. She too, had her life planned. I am sure she didn't relish the thought of what Joseph, her fiance, would say when he learned that she was pregnant. Yet she said yes. She was filled with a lasting joy, one that carried her to the home of her cousin, Elizabeth, where she would proclaim, "My soul magnifies the Lord and my spirit exults in God my savior!"

Jesus doesn't force you. That's what the old Episcopalian priest told me when I was struggling with accepting a ministry of healing, and after all these years, I know it to be true. Jesus never forces. He simply asks. Almighty God stands before someone he created from nothing and humbly asks for love, for service, for obedience.

As we walked out of church that day, I told Ingrid and Jill that I would not be going home to Ireland. I phoned my Tampa convent and Ireland to let them know of my decision. Then I went about the work of the ministry.

Several weeks later, I decided to call home to speak to a girlfriend who is like a sister to me. Thinking my aunt had died, I asked my friend, "Betty, how are things?"

"You mean you haven't heard?" she asked surprised and immediately told me my aunt was alive much to the surprise of everyone, including her doctor.

Then Betty told me the story about the day Auntie Lizzie was supposed to be dying, the very day that I had decided not to return home, but to obey the Lord.

The doctor stood over her bed, talking to a nurse. He was saying that Auntie Lizzie was in a coma and she had a short time to live.

Suddenly, Auntie Lizzie opened her eyes and said, "Well, doctor, how are you and how is your ailing daughter?"

The doctor was so shocked, he ran out of the room and sent another nurse in to check on my aunt.

As the nurse entered the room, Auntie Lizzie pointed to a No Smoking sign and said, "Now, dearie, would you turn that sign around and get me a wee cup of tea and a cigarette? I'm dying for tea and a cigarette." Auntie Lizzie was far from dead!

As Betty was telling me this great news on the phone, I heard Jesus whisper in my other ear, "So Briege, did you really think you could outdo me in generosity?"

After I finished in Brazil, since Auntie Lizzie was still critically ill, I went home to see her. I walked into the hospital room and said, "Auntie Lizzie, I'm home to see you."

She looked at me and said, "I know and it's about time. I waited seven weeks for you to come." Then she pulled me down and whispered to me, "I was going to Jesus and I was ready to go, but he told me, 'No, Lizzie, I want you to wait for Briege to come home, and then I'll take you.'"

Then she said to me, "Now, you've seen me alive, and I can't live forever. Say a wee prayer for me and for these others"—and she told me what was wrong with everybody else in the ward— "and then go back to America and do for Jesus what you promised to do for him."

She kissed me and I left. Two days after I got back to Tampa, Auntie Lizzie went home to the Lord. When I got the news she had died, I was ready to leave for a mission in New Orleans. I remember the great joy I felt and I could hear the Lord saying, "You can never know my generosity if you yourself will not put me first."

I have another story that emphasizes the importance of

trusting the Lord and abandoning yourself to him. I was in Rome during the 1977 Synod of Bishops. Cardinal Suenens had invited some of us to come to Rome to intercede with the Lord for the bishops as they discussed matters concerning the church. While at dinner my first evening in Rome, my wallet was stolen from my handbag. I lost my traveler's checks, about $300 cash, my driver's license, and some photographs that were very dear to me.

I've given many talks about trusting God and putting all your trust in him, because he will never abandon you. Those are beautiful words; but it's one thing to tell people to trust God, and it's another thing to be tested on it.

Margie Grace was with us in Rome. She had advised me to watch out for pickpockets. I went to Margie's room and knocked on the door. My face must have told my story, because as she opened the door, she looked at me and said, "You've been robbed."

Margie consoled me. In many ways she has been like a mother to me over the years, giving me sound advice and praying for me. The next day we went down to the police station to report the missing wallet. Of course, I couldn't describe the thief. I didn't know who had stolen my wallet and other things out of my handbag, but I knew it happened when a band of gypsies began harassing us in the restaurant.

The story got around and everyone said they were praying for me and telling me to trust in the Lord, that he would care for me. I believed that, but I couldn't help thinking, "But I haven't seen one red cent yet."

The Lord, however, was working. A Franciscan priest, Fr. Dermot Ryan, went on a pilgrimage from Ireland to Rome and Assisi. Many things happened when he got there. When he got to Assisi, there was a train strike so he couldn't spend his money on a train ticket. Someone agreed to take him back to Rome, but they refused to be paid any money. The place where he was staying wouldn't take money. He said to himself, looking at this envelope of money, "No matter who I offer the money to, I can't get rid of it."

At mass that day, in the Basilica of St. Clare, he got a strong message that the money was for me. He didn't even know I was in Rome. When he arrived in Rome, he heard I was there, got my address, and came to see me.

When I came to the main desk in the hotel, he handed me an envelope and said, "Briege, I received a word that this money is for you." I opened the envelope to discover it contained, almost to the penny, the amount of money that had been stolen from me.

That wasn't the end of the Lord's generosity. Of course, my traveler's checks had been refunded; on top of that, Margie Grace decided, in her generosity, to get me some more traveler's checks just in case something would happen. I ended up leaving Rome with more money than I had brought into Rome, even though I had been robbed. Cardinal Suenens said, when I shared the testimony with our group of intercessors, "Don't make it a habit of being robbed, because it doesn't always happen like this!"

These two experiences had happy endings but in the process they tested my trust in the Lord. The Lord had a rather painful lesson in store for me to teach me the meaning and value of the cross.

Carrying the Cross

Jesus told the disciples they must take up their crosses and follow him. That is true for us today. In our commitment, we will encounter sorrows. We will encounter the cross.

Today, people want to make commitments on their terms. Because they will not rely on Jesus and trust him, they fail to realize his protection and generosity. In all walks of life, we see this "qualified commitment" or "conditional commitment." Neither is really commitment. It is especially noticeable and tragic in marriage, where people enter a relationship with the idea that if it doesn't work out, they will walk out. Such a relationship doesn't stand a chance.

Some people misunderstand the place of the cross in the Christian life. Sometimes they believe Christianity promises escape from discomfort, displeasure, poverty, pain, and frustration. This kind of spirituality ignores Jesus' explicit statement that we will be persecuted and his direction that we take up our crosses if we want to follow him.

In my own life, while I gave my life to Jesus, there were moments of suffering, moments I had to struggle through temptation, through disappointments, rejection and misunderstanding, great challenges, and inevitable suffering.

The most vivid experience of challenge to faith and of bearing my own cross came to me in the death of my father.

My father was a strong man, a farmer. He died unexpectedly one winter night as he came home from visiting with friends. As he walked up the steps of his home and started to open the door, he had a stroke. All night he lay there, alone and helpless, unable to call for help, with my brother and his family just across the street. He was discovered dead the next morning. He had frozen to death.

My father died just as I was beginning a period of rest and reflection at the home of Doris and Francis Meagher, two very dear friends, in Clearwater, Florida. I went to Ireland for the funeral.

As I thought about my father's death, I wondered how this could have happened. I had stood by the beds of many dying people, comforting them, and helping them prepare to see Jesus. But for my own father to die as he did, alone and without family near him, with my brother's home in full view but no one to comfort him—how could this be?

Because of my faith in Jesus, I could look at death as a believer must. It is only an opening of a door. The way he died was tragic, but on the other hand, he could have been lying for years in unbearable pain. The Lord took him through the door of death more quickly than that—and took him as he lived, on his way with his key in his hand. He is now with the Lord and that is far better than anything we can have on earth.

From this experience, I realized that death is like being born. When a baby is in the womb, it is safe and secure. If a baby could talk, I am sure it would say it doesn't want to leave the womb, that it would rather not take the chance to see what the world is all about because there is no coming back. With our belief in eternal life, we can see the world as a womb, a womb preparing us for a birth into a new life. We, like the baby, don't want to go through the door of death into that other life. It is an unknown, there is no returning. Even with faith, we hesitate to take that plunge. Yet any person who has gone through the door of death into the arms of Jesus would say they would never come back.

With all of that, my faith and this deeper understanding of death, it did not make my sorrow any easier. When I left home to return to the United States to start my mission to Brazil, a wave of sorrow and loneliness hit me. I remember that in Dublin, as I was waiting to leave, Father Kevin just sat with me as I cried. I just had to let out the sorrow. I had to be able to express this sorrow. Some people do not understand that sorrow is a natural emotion that must be expressed. Because this good friend could listen and let me cry, I felt the Lord's strength coming to me through him as friend, believer, and priest.

I was able to offer this suffering to the Lord as my prayer and preparation for my ministry in Brazil. Because I was so empty, because I had to rely on him totally, because I accepted my brokenness and humanity, Jesus was able to reach his people through me in many beautiful ways.

The Victory of Faithfulness

Out of the suffering in my life, I did get a teaching about how we can't avoid the cross.

We also express faith in the victory of the cross and in resurrection through commitments we make in daily life, such as in marriage and in our relationships to religious superiors and others.

There are many ways in which my commitment to Jesus is expressed. For me, as a religious, I see it expressed through my vows and to my commitment to the Congregation of St. Clare. The Sisters of St. Clare are my new and spiritual family, the family of St. Clare.

We women have committed our lives to fulfill our vocations to holiness and celibacy, sharing the same life. My commitment to him and to my congregation affects not only my life, but theirs as well. In fact, it affects the broader church as well, through prayer, witness, and ministry.

Family members affect one another's lives. They call each other to holiness and they challenge one another. This is true for both natural families and families of religious. I have an obligation to be committed, to live up to that commitment and to remain close to my congregation. I do this in two ways.

First, I travel a lot and I am not always present in my community. I must share my experiences with the community. They have a right to this because, through prayer, and through the mutuality and unity born of our life as religious, they are part of my ministry as I am a part of theirs.

I do not go into the world on my own. They send me out, in the name of the whole congregation. What any of us does is done in the spirit and under the direction of the community and of the superiors who serve the community by giving direction and calling forth gifts, all in the light of our vision of service in and to the church, for the glory of God.

Second, I remain close to my community through my vow of obedience. I have to submit myself—and all the voices and images I've mentioned in this book—to the discernment of my mother general and her advisors.

I don't just roam around the world at random, simply because I think God told me to do so. I always tell my mother general what I think God is saying to me, but I am totally submissive to her decisions. Most of the time, I get approval for what I believe I should do, but sometimes approval is withheld. Several years ago, I was invited to Australia. I told my mother general, expecting her to give her permission as usual. However, this time she said, "After prayer, I don't think you should go to Australia. It isn't the right time."

Normally a person would ask, "Why? It looks like a good idea. They need to hear the gospel there in Australia."

But I believed what the great St. Catherine said, that you can always make a mistake, that you cannot be sure you're hearing God when you hear voices, but that you can always ask your mother superior to repeat what she said so you can be sure she meant what you heard her say. That's what's good about obedience. You can always make sure you're hearing right.

I accepted her decision as God's will. Three weeks later, in California, I met Agnes Sanford, the great pioneer of the healing ministry in the Anglican church. While she was praying with me she got a word from the Lord. I had told her nothing about Australia, but she said, "The time for you to go to Australia isn't now. God will bring you to Australia, but it is not in his plan for you to go now, and he wants you to feel at ease with what you have already been told."

I told her about my mother general. Her response was, "Isn't it marvelous to recognize God working through obedience?"

I truly agree with that statement. Obedience is not something that smothers people. Obedience frees people. It is not something that weakens people; it empowers them. Obedience ennobles the body of a community. The authority of a superior rests in the community.

Consider the story of the centurion. He said Jesus didn't have to go to where his servant boy was to heal him. All Jesus had to do was command that the boy be healed and he would be healed. He told Jesus, "I, too, am a man under authority. And when I say come, they come; when I say go, they go. Speak but the word and my serving boy shall be healed" (Mt 8:8-9).

The centurion realized that when he was in obedience to the emperor, he had the emperor's authority. He could do many things in the name of the emperor. So it was with Jesus. Because

Jesus, as a human being, was totally committed to and obedient to the Father, he had the Father's power. He could heal. He could bring the dead to life. He could give sight to the blind and cure lepers and the lame. Nothing was impossible to Jesus, because through obedience, he was vested with the full power and authority of the Father.

So it is with Christians who obey the Lord. That is why the Lord can preach, teach, heal, comfort, and admonish through his people—because the church is obedient to the Lord. If Christians truly believe what Jesus taught, they will obey the church, because the church has the very authority of Jesus to pastor, guide, and govern the Christians of the world.

As I said earlier, as a sister of St. Clare, I am obedient to the Lord whom I know and love personally. He loves me and reveals himself to me. Yet, I could not have a healing ministry, as a sister of St. Clare, if I did not submit to his authority as expressed through my superior. Nor could I have a healing ministry, as a sister of St. Clare, if I saw myself separate from my community of sisters. I cannot serve as a sister of St. Clare if I cease to be a sister of St. Clare. One benefit of the vow of obedience is that it helps all of us to measure our own vision against the community's vision. Authority, properly exercised and revered, is a source of unity, strength, and power.

The same is true for married people. There must be mutual respect and love in a marriage. Every Christian marriage has a mission to make Jesus present in the world. Husband and wife must constantly check their individual inspirations with the other, to protect the unity, the vision, the impact of their love on society and on the church.

We celebrate faith by being faithful. There is no other way. Exercising our faith is a celebration of it. When people are in love, they marry, and in the union of their spirits and bodies, they celebrate love.

We have faith, and we celebrate that faith by clinging, with love and commitment, to the object of that faith, Jesus the

Lord. For Jesus, the ultimate word of love is his cross. For us, the ultimate word of love for Jesus is doing his will, regardless of the cost, which is often, for us, a cross.

A Signpost to Jesus

In closing this book, I want to remind everyone of something I said earlier. You've read here a lot about my kind of prayer, my kind of spirituality, my images, and small voices. Please don't think you are supposed to experience what I experience.

God speaks to each of us in his own way. I happen to have a vivid imagination and a love for stories. God uses that to help me communicate faith. There are many saints in our history, and in the world today, who simply do not, cannot, and don't want to hear voices or see images or visions.

Many saints go through life with very few "goosebump experiences." The great St. Teresa complained about long periods of spiritual dryness in which she never consciously experienced the presence of God or any form of spiritual consolation.

Don't model yourself on anyone. As Mother Angelica says, "The best way to pray is the way you pray best."

I want to close this book with two things. First, I believe that in 1 Timothy 6:12-16 we find a beautiful ending to this discussion on obedience. I also believe it helps us understand better what it means to be a "signpost to Jesus."

Second, I have asked my coauthor, Henry Libersat, to write an epilogue that will share how God has worked in his life since we first met and prayed ten years ago.

I pray that this book will help us all grow in faith and become more aware of the importance of living in the Lord, by the Lord, for the Lord. I pray that all of you will pray for one another and especially for everyone in ministry, including myself. I ask that you all please pray for priests, that you revere the church and stay close to the sacraments.

As Christians we are called to be a sign of the presence of God. Through faith and obedience, in the Spirit sent by Jesus, we have great power and the call and opportunity to do much good in the world and to bring souls to God.

Please pray that in my ministry I will always be a signpost to Jesus.

Fight the good fight of faith. Take firm hold on the everlasting life to which you were called when, in the presence of many witnesses, you made your noble profession of faith. Before God, who gives life to all, and before Christ Jesus, who in bearing witness made his noble profession before Pontius Pilate, I charge you to keep God's command without blame or reproach until our Lord Jesus Christ shall appear. This appearance God will bring to pass at his chosen time. He is the blessed and only ruler, the King of kings and Lord of lords who alone has immortality and who dwells in unapproachable light, whom no human being has ever seen or can see. To him be honor and everlasting rule! Amen.

(1 Tm 6:12-16)

Epilogue

WHEN I FIRST HEARD about Sister Briege McKenna, O.S.C., in 1974, I was very skeptical. However, as editor of *The Florida Catholic,* a weekly paper that covers five of Florida's seven dioceses, I had many opportunities to read stories about her.

In the summer of 1976, when I was forty-two years of age, one of our reporters did another story on Sister Briege's ministry. I was moved to write her to ask for prayer.

That year, I was coming to grips with some very important questions in my life. I was beginning to question whether I really had faith in Jesus Christ, whether I believed he was alive and truly cared what happened to me. I had been in the Catholic press seventeen years and was going to Sunday mass regularly. I had taught CCD and was generally recognized as a "fine Catholic man."

But I was unhappy and was beginning to realize I was suffering from alcoholism.

I saw many Catholic people whose lives were renewed through prayer and they were speaking about miracles and healings. I had always wondered why, if this is indeed the same church as in the time of Jesus and the apostles, there were no miracles in our day.

Moved by my reporter's story, I wrote Sister Briege and told her I felt I had a barrier inside, keeping me from really knowing God. She wrote back saying she'd pray for me.

Later, I called her, and she prayed with me. All that prayer and no miracles. I didn't feel any closer to God. I was still drinking, although I never told her about that. I wanted a miracle. Why did other people get miracles and not me?

139

Although I was a layman, I preached at Sunday masses on behalf of *The Florida Catholic,* I was scheduled to preach in Tampa, on October 30-31, 1976. I called Sister Briege and she agreed to meet me—something she rarely did—at the church for a private prayer session.

On Sunday morning, after preaching the 10:30 mass homily I walked out of church and met Sister Briege for the first time. She looked normal enough, was dressed in a blue modernized habit, had an easy smile and a certain quality of peace about her. We went into a room behind the church and I told her again that I really wanted to love God and give myself to him.

I remember it well. I've written about it many times, and I've shared the experience throughout Florida, in many places in the United States, and in Brazil and Peru as well. Sister Briege took my hands and said, "Henry, the most difficult thing is to trust."

She explained that we can't even trust people we can see and said, "Henry, how hard it must be for you to trust a God you have never seen."

She prayed a beautiful prayer for my wife Peg and me, for our marriage, and for our children. She asked the Lord to give me "the beautiful gift of prayer."

I began to feel a deep peace spread through me. And she said, "Henry, I see you alone with the Lord and he is in the image of the Sacred Heart. He is saying to you, 'My son, that child that you and your wife have been so worried about and praying for, don't worry about him; my arm is around him and he's all right.'"

Now I was sobbing. I had not told Sister Briege about this child of ours who was having such difficult personal problems.

She continued to pray and said, "Henry, I see you alone with the Lord again and he has his arm around you and he is saying, 'My son, that member of your family who has turned his back on the family, on the church, and has hurt you so much, don't worry about him. My arm's around him and he's all right.'"

Again, I had not told Sister Briege about this relative.

I felt as though there were a bright but gentle light filling my entire being. I knew that God knew me, that he loved me. He knew where I hurt. He revealed himself through Sister Briege, through this tremendous gift of insight, "word of knowledge," or "prophecy"—I don't care what you call it. It is real—and it is a blessing for hurting people, lost people, sick people, searching people, dying people.

Then Sister Briege had another image. "I see you on a mountain top. You are there with the Lord, and on the side of the mountain are many people who want to come up the mountain to be with the Lord. I see you calling to them, but they are frightened and they run behind the rocks and in crevices and shadows and they hide. Henry, the Lord is calling you to a great work."

This was the moment I truly felt the presence of Jesus. I had had many blessings in life: good parents, a great wife, and wonderful kids. I believed in God and was a practicing Catholic, but I had never before been so aware of the power of the baptized soul, of the gentleness and immanence of our God.

I still continued to drink. Sometime during the summer of 1977, I called my friend, Briege. We had indeed become friends by then. I said, "Briege, I never wanted to admit it to you before, but I have a drinking problem."

She immediately began to pray, and she got another one of her images, one that at the moment I wished she had not had. She said, "Henry, I see you walking down a long road. There is a big, deep pit in the road and I see you falling into it. You try to get out, but it's too deep and too steep. Your hands are broken and bleeding. You are so tired you can't stand and you fall down, and roll over on your back. With your last ounce of strength, I see you raising your hand to heaven and you are pleading to God—and I see his hand come down and lift you from the horrible pit."

There is no need here to go into greater detail. I only want to say that on September 2, 1977, I took my last drink. I went to a

meeting of Alcoholics Anonymous on Sunday, September 4.
That night as I was dozing off, I suddenly jumped up in bed and
exclaimed, "Honey, I'm healed!" Peg said, "Yes, I know."

Life in the Spirit of Jesus has been a tremendously exciting
experience. Peg and I have grown closer, we went through four
years of training, from 1982 to 1986, and then I was ordained a
deacon on Pentecost Sunday, May 18, 1986.

Peg and all but one of our children were there. Several of
Peg's family members were there. My ninety-year-old dad was
there. And Briege was there, next to Peg.

We divide history into B.C. (before Christ) and A.D. (the
year of our Lord). I divide my life B.B. and A.B.—Before Briege
and After Briege.

No greater honor could have been given me than her asking
me to help with this book, *Miracles Do Happen*.

Henry Libersat, Deacon